Copy Editor & Interior Design: Constance Santego
Book Layout: ©2017 BookDesignTemplates.com

Ordering Information:
Quantity sales. Special discounts are available on quantity purchases by corporations, associations, and others. For details, contact the "Special Sales Department" at the address above.

Trade Paperback ISBN: 978-1-990062-94-0
eBook ISBN 978-1-990062-95-7
Created and published In Canada. Printed and bound in the United States of America

First Edition
Published by Maximillian Enterprises
Kelowna, BC Canada
www.constancesantego.ca

# Root Chakra 101: Building Safety, Survival, Foundation

*"Reconnect with the earth, reclaim your foundation, and rise with stability."*

(Vol II)

Dr. Constance Santego

Maximillian Enterprises
Kelowna, BC

# *Dedication*

For the healers, seekers, and teachers who walk the path of grounding and safety. May this guide help you stand firm in your own roots, even as you support others in finding theirs.

— Dr. Constance Santego

# ALSO BY DR. CONSTANCE SANTEGO

**NOVELS**
Illegitimate Grace
Ashcroft Hollow

**Okanagan Trilogy:**
Beneath the Vineyards
Under the Okanagan Sun
Guardian of the Lake

**The Nine Spiritual Gifts Series:**
Journey of a Soul – (Vol 1 Michael)
Language of a Soul – (Vol 2 Gabriel)
Prophecy of a Soul – (Vol 3 Bath Kol)
Healing of a Soul – (Vol 4 Raphael)
Miracles of a Soul – (Vol 5 Hamied)
Knowledge of a Soul – (Vol 6 Raziel)
Wisdom of a Soul – (Vol 7 Uriel)
Faith of a Soul – (Vol 8 Pistis Sophia)

**NONFICTION**
The Intuitive Life, The Gift Of Prophecy, Third Edition
Fairy Tales, Dreams And Reality… Where Are You On Your Path? Second Edition
Your Persona… The Mask You Wear
Archangel Michael's Soul Retrieval Guide
Tesla And The Future Of Energy Medicine
Beyond Tesla: Advancing The Science Of Energy Healing
Tesla's Code: Mastering Energy, Frequency, And Creative Power
Beyond The Mind: Harnessing The Power Of Astral Projection For Creative Awakening
Bend, Don't Break: Finding Your Way Back To Abundance
Ring Therapy: A Guide To Healing And Balance
Ring Therapy Pocket Guide
Floraopathy™: The Art And Science Of Vibrational Healing With Essential Oils
Dear Older Me: A Memoir… Of Sorts
It's Just Like Poker: A Spiritual Guide To Playing The Cards Life Deals You
Signs And Meanings: What The Feet Reveal About Health, Stress, And The Body's Story
Auricions: Unlocking Subconscious Healing Through Quantum Medicine
Quick Fix Acupressure Method
Manifestation – The DREAM Method in 5 Steps
Confidence- Mastering the Dream Method

**REIKI WISDOM, SERIES:**
Angelic Lifestyle, a Vibrant Lifestyle
Angelic Lifestyle 42-Day Energy Cleanse
Reiki and the Power of The Joint Points: Unlocking Energy Pathways for Healing (Vol I)
*Reiki and Karmic Healing: Releasing Patterns From Past Lives* (Vol II)
Reiki and the Five Elements (Vol III)
Secrets of a Healer, Magic Of Reiki
The Reiki Master's Manual

**CHAKRA SERIES:**
Heart Chakra 101: The Bridge
Root Chakra 101: Building Safety, Survival, Foundation
Sacral Chakra 101: Creativity, Pleasure, Emotions
Solar Plexus Chakra 101: Power, Confidence, Will
Throat Chakra 101: Truth, Voice, Self-Expression
Third Eye Chakra 10: Intuition, Vision, Insight
Crown Chakra 10: Spiritual Connection, Transcendence.

**SECRETS OF A HEALER, SERIES:**
Magic Of Aromatherapy (Vol I)
Magic Of Reflexology (Vol II)
Magic Of The Gifts (Vol III)
Magic Of Muscle Testing (Vol IV)
Magic Of Iridology (Vol V)
Magic Of Massage (Vol VI)
Magic Of Hypnotherapy (Vol VII)
Magic Of Reiki (Vol VIII)
Magic Of Advanced Aromatherapy (Vol IX)
Magic Of Esthetics (Vol X)
The Reiki Master's Manual (Vol XI)

**ADULT COLORING JOURNALS**
SERIES-ZEN COLORING:
Quantum Energy and Mindful Living Journal (Vol 1)
Reiki Energy Journal (Vol 2)
Nine Spiritual Gifts Journal (Vol 3)
I Forgive Journal (Vol 4)

**FOR CHILDREN**
I am Big Tonight. I Don't Need the Light
The Magic Elf Book: 25 Days of Surprises

**COOKBOOK**
My Favorite Recipes, with a Hint of Giggle

**BUISNESS**
How To Use ChatGPT For Authors: From Idea To Published Book
Scaling Beyond 6 Figures: Strategies For Health & Wellness Professionals
The Academypreneur's Playbook: Turn Knowledge Into A
Revenue-Generating School

**HUMOR/GIFT BOOK**
How Do You Like Your Eggs? Crack Into Your Personality, Yolk and All

# Contents

# Preface

## Introduction: Returning to the Ground of Being

When we began our journey with the Heart Chakra, we stepped into the center of the human energy system — the bridge between body and spirit, earth and sky, self and other. The heart teaches us compassion, connection, and the power of love. Yet even love needs a place to land. Without a steady ground beneath it, even the most open heart can falter.

This is where the Root Chakra, or **Muladhara**, enters the story. Located at the base of the spine, Muladhara is the foundation of the chakra system. It governs our sense of safety, stability, and belonging — the deep assurance that we have a place in this world, that our bodies are supported, and that life can be trusted. Where the heart asks us to give and receive freely, the root asks us to stand, breathe, and claim space on the earth.

The body reflects this truth. The heart may expand the chest, inviting us to reach out to others, but the root anchors us through the legs, feet, bones, and muscles. The pulse of survival and the instinct to ground flow through this chakra. When Muladhara is balanced, we feel centered, resilient, and supported. When it is imbalanced, fear, insecurity, and instability ripple upward, unsettling the entire system — even the heart.

In this way, the **heart and root are inseparable partners**. One opens us to love, while the other ensures we feel safe enough to live and share that love. Just as a tree can only reach toward the sun when its roots are firmly planted in the earth, our capacity for connection, compassion, and spiritual awakening depends on the strength of our foundation.

This book is an invitation to explore that foundation. Together we will uncover the wisdom of the Root Chakra: its symbols and stories, its shadows and strengths, and its practical tools for healing and balance. Through reflection, energy practices, and connection with the earth itself, you will learn how to restore your ground of being — and from that ground, rise into life with confidence, security, and presence.

# Chapter 1 – Entering the Ground of Being

## The Role of the Root Chakra in the Chakra System

Every journey begins with a first step, and in the energetic body, that step is taken through the Root Chakra, **Muladhara**. Though this series began at the heart — the bridge of love and balance — it is here, at the base of the spine, that the energy system finds its anchor.

The Root Chakra is the **foundation of all the chakras**. Just as a house cannot stand without a stable base, our energy cannot rise without the security of grounding. Muladhara connects us to the physical world — to earth, to family, to survival. It is the energy of birth, of being carried into existence, of knowing that life itself will sustain us.

While the Heart Chakra teaches connection, the Root Chakra teaches **safety and belonging**. It whispers: *You are allowed to be here. You have a place on this earth. You are supported.* Without this inner assurance, the higher chakras struggle to remain steady. Fear, anxiety, or instability at the root can ripple upward, clouding our emotions, thoughts, and even spiritual insight.

Muladhara is associated with the **element of earth**, the heaviest and most grounding of all the elements. Its color is deep red — the color of blood, clay, and primal vitality. Its symbol, the four-petaled lotus with a downward-pointing triangle, reminds us that all energy must eventually return to the ground. It is both the beginning and the constant support of our spiritual ascent.

In the chakra system, each energy center builds upon the one before it. The Root gives rise to the Sacral (creativity), the Solar Plexus (power), the Heart (love), the Throat (truth), the Third Eye (vision), and the Crown (spirit). If the Root is weak, the rest of the system trembles; if it is strong, everything above it can flourish.

Think of Muladhara as the **roots of a great tree**. The branches and leaves may stretch toward the light, but it is the hidden roots that keep the tree alive through storms, droughts, and seasons of change. In the same way, your Root Chakra is the hidden strength that allows you to grow, heal, and reach toward your highest potential.

Muladhara is both **the beginning and the support of the journey.** It is the first chakra to form in early childhood, carrying the memory of safety or instability into all later experiences. It is also the ever-present foundation that holds us steady no matter how high we climb in consciousness. Without Muladhara, the entire chakra system is unrooted, like a tree without soil. With it, we gain the strength to stand tall, endure hardship, and rise toward spiritual awakening with confidence.

In this way, Muladhara is not simply a starting point — it is a **constant companion**. Every step we take in healing, every moment of spiritual growth, is supported by this chakra. As we expand upward toward vision and transcendence, Muladhara keeps us rooted, reminding us that enlightenment is not escape but embodiment.

## SANSKRIT NAME

- **Muladhara (मूलाधार)** – the original name from yogic texts.
  - *Mula* = root
  - *Adhara* = support, foundation
  - Literal meaning: **"Root Support" or "Foundation."**
    This is the most authentic and traditional name.

## COMMON ENGLISH NAMES

- **Root Chakra** – the most widely used name today, especially in yoga, Reiki, and New Age traditions. Emphasizes grounding and the imagery of roots connecting us to earth.
- **Base Chakra** – another popular translation, especially in early Theosophical writings (C.W. Leadbeater, Alice Bailey) and in British/Australian traditions. Highlights its position at the base of the spine.

## THE DIFFERENCE BETWEEN "ROOT CHAKRA" AND "BASE CHAKRA"

Mostly comes from translation, cultural adaptation, and preference in different healing traditions — but they refer to the same energy center: Muladhara.

Here's the breakdown:

**Sanskrit Term**

- The original Sanskrit name is **Muladhara** (mula = root, adhara = support/foundation).
- This literally means "root support" or "foundation."

## Western Translation Variations

- **"Root Chakra"**: Became common in Western yoga, Reiki, and New Age teachings. The word "root" emphasizes its connection to grounding, survival, and being anchored to the earth.
- **"Base Chakra"**: More often used in early Theosophical writings (like C.W. Leadbeater) and sometimes in British/Australian traditions. It highlights the chakra's location at the *base of the spine* as the physical foundation of the chakra system.

## Symbolic Nuance

- **Root Chakra** evokes imagery of a tree's roots — depth, nourishment, stability, connection to earth. It feels more organic and metaphorical.
- **Base Chakra** emphasizes position — the literal bottom of the energy system, the starting point or first rung of the ladder.

## Modern Usage

- Most modern yoga, meditation, and chakra healing books use the **Root Chakra** because it ties into the symbolic language of grounding and "rooting."
- Some Reiki or Western energy healing texts still say **Base Chakra**, especially when presenting chakras as a sequence (base → sacral → solar plexus, etc.).

**Both are correct** — it's more about tone and audience. If you're writing for readers who resonate with **holistic, spiritual, and symbolic** language, "Root Chakra" feels warmer and more alive. If you're aiming for a **clinical or technical** feel, "Base Chakra" may sound more anatomical.

## OTHER TRANSLATIONS & DESCRIPTIONS

- **First Chakra** – simple numbering in modern chakra teachings.
- **Foundation Chakra** – less common, but sometimes used to highlight its role as the energetic base for the rest of the system.
- **Earth Chakra** – occasionally used in energy healing or elemental frameworks because of its association with the earth element (Prithvi).
- **Root Center / Base Center** – phrasing sometimes found in Western esoteric or psychological interpretations.

## IN ESOTERIC/HEALING CONTEXTS

- Some practitioners describe Muladhara as the **"seat of Kundalini"** because it is said to be where the serpent energy lies dormant, coiled three and a half times at the base of the spine.
- In certain mystical frameworks, it's also referred to as the **"gateway to incarnation"** since it is tied to birth, survival, and entry into the material world.

# Muladhara: The Foundation of Human Experience

The Sanskrit name for the Root Chakra is **Muladhara**, a word that carries deep meaning. *Mula* translates to "root" or "origin," while *adhara* means "support" or "foundation." Together they reveal the essence of this chakra: **the root that supports life itself**.

From the moment of birth, our survival depends on the qualities of Muladhara. Breathing, eating, finding shelter, and feeling safe — these primal needs are not distractions from spiritual life; they are the bedrock upon which all growth is built. Just as a seed must first take root in the soil before it can grow toward the light, we too must feel grounded in our bodies and in the world before higher states of awareness can unfold.

Muladhara represents the **instinctive wisdom of the body**. It is the part of us that knows how to find balance, to fight or flee when threatened, to rest when tired, to seek nourishment when hungry. Often overlooked in favor of more "spiritual" centers, this chakra is a reminder that spirit cannot thrive without form, and consciousness cannot expand without a vessel strong enough to hold it.

When Muladhara is balanced, life feels stable and trustworthy. We move with confidence, we know where our next meal will come from, and we feel connected to the earth beneath our feet. When it is imbalanced, fear becomes our constant companion: fear of scarcity, fear of not belonging, fear of being unsafe in our own skin. These fears ripple upward, affecting emotions, thoughts, and relationships, making it difficult to feel peace in the heart or clarity in the mind.

In this way, Muladhara is not only the beginning of the chakra system but the **foundation of human experience**. Without grounding, the entire energetic structure wobbles. With grounding, every other chakra has the strength to blossom.

Just as a tree's roots remain unseen but hold the power of life within them, your root chakra is the quiet, unseen energy that keeps you alive, safe, and whole. It is here, in the red earth of Muladhara, that your journey into survival, security, and belonging truly begins.

# What Is Sanskrit and Why Does It Matter for Chakras?

The language most often associated with the chakras is **Sanskrit**, an ancient Indian language considered by many to be a language of vibration. Each chakra's name in Sanskrit not only identifies it but also carries an energetic quality that reflects the essence of the chakra itself.

For the Root Chakra, the Sanskrit name is **Muladhara**. *Mula* means "root," and *adhara* means "support" or "foundation." Together, the word embodies the role of this chakra as the grounding structure for human life. Unlike a simple label, Sanskrit words are designed to be **felt as much as spoken** — their sound vibration influences the body and energy field.

Sanskrit is significant for chakras because it preserves a system of **sacred sound**. Each chakra has a *bija mantra* (seed sound) that activates and resonates with its energy. For Muladhara, the sound is **LAM**. When spoken, sung, or chanted, "LAM" generates a low, grounding vibration that can be felt in the body, especially at the base of the spine. In this way, the sound itself becomes a healing tool, harmonizing the energy of the chakra.

Sanskrit also provides a symbolic framework. The **letters of the Sanskrit alphabet** are often depicted on the lotus petals of chakra mandalas, reinforcing the idea that language, vibration, and consciousness are inseparable. The four petals of Muladhara's lotus carry four Sanskrit syllables, each tied to qualities of stability and support.

Why does this matter today? Because language shapes consciousness. By using the Sanskrit name, sound, and symbolism of Muladhara, we tap into thousands of years of wisdom that recognized the body as more than physical flesh —

it is a temple of vibration. Speaking or meditating on Sanskrit words is not about cultural formality, but about entering a relationship with the **energetic essence of being human**.

When you chant "LAM," you're not just repeating a sound. You're affirming: *I am here. I am safe. I am rooted in the earth.*

# The Root Chakra and Maslow's Hierarchy of Needs

In the 20th century, psychologist Abraham Maslow introduced his **Hierarchy of Needs**, a framework describing the stages of human motivation. At the base of his pyramid lie the *physiological needs* — food, water, sleep, shelter — followed by *safety needs*, such as protection, stability, and security. Only when these are met can a person move upward toward belonging, esteem, and ultimately self-actualization.

This modern psychological model beautifully mirrors the **chakra system**. Just as Maslow saw basic needs as the foundation of human growth, the ancient yogis recognized that without balance in the Root Chakra, the higher chakras cannot fully awaken.

- **Root Chakra ↔ Physiological & Safety Needs**
  The Root governs survival, health, and the assurance of safety. If we feel insecure in our body or environment, our energy cannot rise to the higher chakras.
- **Sacral Chakra ↔ Belonging & Relationships**
  Once safety is established, we can explore creativity, sexuality, and emotional bonds.
- **Solar Plexus ↔ Esteem & Personal Power**
  Confidence, willpower, and self-worth come when the foundation below is strong.

- **Heart Chakra ↔ Love & Connection**
  Compassion and unconditional love require that we already feel safe, worthy, and capable of giving and receiving.
- **Throat Chakra ↔ Self-Expression**
  With belonging and love in place, we can speak our truth.
- **Third Eye ↔ Insight & Vision**
  Higher awareness unfolds when the lower needs no longer consume our energy.
- **Crown Chakra ↔ Self-Actualization & Transcendence**
  Maslow's highest level aligns with spiritual awakening, connection to the divine, and the realization of unity.

Seen this way, the chakra system and Maslow's hierarchy are **two maps of the same journey**: one rooted in ancient India, the other in modern psychology. Both teach us that the path to wholeness begins with **grounded survival and safety**. We cannot reach for the stars without first planting our feet firmly on the earth.

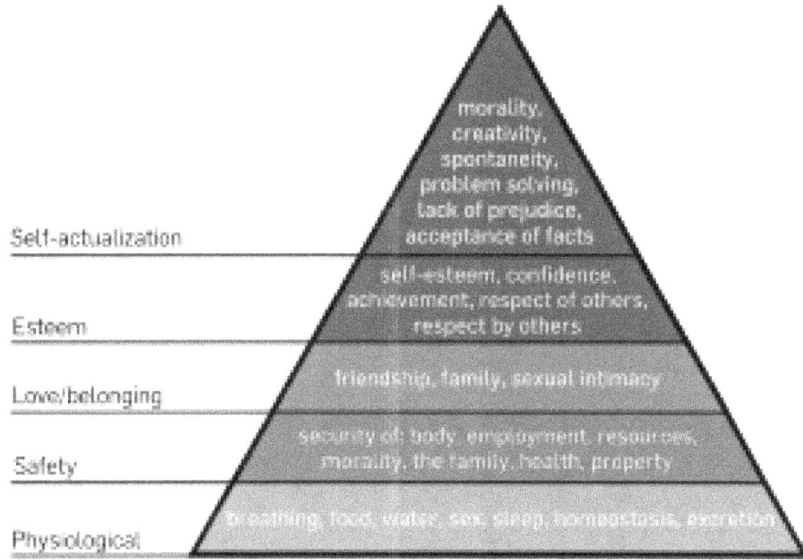

**Mazlow's Hierarchy of Needs**

## ROOT CHAKRA ↔ PHYSIOLOGICAL & SAFETY NEEDS

The **Root Chakra (Muladhara)** is the foundation of the entire chakra system, just as **physiological and safety needs** form the base of Maslow's hierarchy. Without stability at this level, neither psychological growth nor spiritual awakening can unfold fully.

### Physiological Needs: Survival of the Body

At its most fundamental, the Root Chakra governs the body's instinctual drive to survive. This includes the biological functions and resources required for life itself:

- **Food and Water**: Nourishment sustains not only the body but also the energy system. Malnourishment or dehydration weakens the root.
- **Sleep and Rest**: Adequate rest restores the adrenal system, which is directly linked with Muladhara. Chronic exhaustion depletes root energy.
- **Shelter and Warmth**: Protection from the elements gives a sense of physical safety. Without it, fear dominates, weakening the foundation.
- **Breath and Elimination**: The simplest bodily rhythms—breathing, digestion, elimination—are root-level processes that anchor us in the material world.

When these needs are unmet, the Root Chakra contracts, creating feelings of fear, scarcity, and insecurity. Energy cannot ascend to higher chakras if the body is preoccupied with survival.

### Safety Needs: Security of Body and Environment

Beyond raw survival, Muladhara is equally tied to the **assurance of safety**. This includes both physical and psychological security:

- **Health and Vitality**: Feeling strong in the body gives confidence to move through life. Chronic illness, weakness, or instability creates an imbalance.
- **Financial Stability**: While not traditionally discussed in yogic texts, modern life ties survival to income. A lack of financial grounding can trigger root insecurity.
- **Consistency and Routine**: Predictable rhythms (day/night cycles, stable relationships, a safe home) provide the structure that mirrors Muladhara's stability.
- **Personal and Community Safety**: Living in a violent or unstable environment agitates the Root Chakra, keeping the nervous system in constant fight-or-flight mode.

**Why This Matters for Energy Flow**

Just as Maslow's hierarchy shows that unmet physiological and safety needs halt higher development, the chakra system teaches that blocked root energy prevents the natural upward flow through the chakras. If Muladhara is weak or unstable:

- The **Sacral Chakra (Svadhisthana)** struggles to feel safe enough to explore pleasure, creativity, or intimacy.
- The **Solar Plexus (Manipura)** cannot fully develop confidence or personal power.
- The **Heart Chakra (Anahata)** may struggle to open, as love requires a sense of safety and belonging at the base level.

When the Root Chakra is nourished, the entire system thrives. A balanced root provides the sense of **"I am safe, I am supported, I belong here."** Only with this assurance can energy rise toward growth, self-expression, and spiritual awakening.

# Chapter 2 – Foundations of Muladhara

## Root Chakra Basics: A Gentle Recap

If you are new to chakra study, the Root Chakra, or **Muladhara**, is the first of the seven main chakras. It is located at the base of the spine, in the perineum area, and extends downward like energetic roots connecting you to the earth.

The energy here is primal and instinctual. It governs the **will to live, to survive, and to feel safe in the body and the world**. Just as a tree must send its roots deep into the ground before it can grow tall, Muladhara gives us the stability and nourishment needed to support all other chakras above it.

**Key qualities of Muladhara include:**

- **Element:** Earth — solid, grounding, stabilizing.
- **Color:** Deep red — the color of blood, clay, and the life force that sustains us.
- **Symbol:** A four-petaled lotus containing a square and a downward-facing triangle, representing grounding, stability, and the pull of gravity.
- **Sound (Bija Mantra):** LAM — the seed syllable that resonates with the vibration of safety and rootedness.
- **Location in the body:** Base of the spine, pelvic floor, legs, feet, and bones.
- **Organs and systems:** Adrenal glands, skeletal structure, colon, elimination system, and immune defenses.

- • **Core themes:** Survival, stability, security, belonging, family, tribe, and connection to the earth.

When Muladhara is **balanced**, you feel steady, secure, and present. Your basic needs — food, shelter, health, and safety — are acknowledged and tended to, and you move through life with confidence and trust.

When it is **blocked or weak**, you may feel anxious, ungrounded, or chronically insecure. Fear of scarcity, instability in relationships, or disconnection from the body are common.

When it is **overactive**, energy may become rigid, controlling, or overly materialistic. Instead of feeling rooted, you may cling to possessions, status, or routines out of fear of losing stability.

Muladhara is the reminder that spirituality is not about escaping the body — it is about **living fully in it**. By tending to the root, you give yourself the gift of being present, embodied, and alive. From this place, you can safely rise into the higher chakras.

# Cross-Cultural Perspectives on the Root

The concept of grounding, safety, and survival energy is not unique to yoga or Sanskrit traditions. Across the world, cultures have identified the importance of being connected to the earth and to the primal life force that sustains us. Though the language and symbols differ, the **essence of Muladhara is universal**: without roots, there can be no growth.

### Yogic Tradition
In the yogic chakra system, Muladhara is the first chakra — the base from which all others arise. It is linked to the earth element, the elephant (a symbol of strength and stability), and the sound *LAM*. Ancient yogis taught that Muladhara houses the dormant energy of **Kundalini**, the serpent coiled three and a

half times at the base of the spine, waiting to awaken. Without a stable root, the ascent of Kundalini can be destabilizing, which is why grounding practices are considered essential.

## Shamanic Traditions
In many shamanic cultures, the concept of being "rooted" is expressed through direct connection with the natural world. Ceremonies often begin by **calling in the four directions** and honoring the earth beneath. Shamans journey into the "lower world," a realm beneath the earth where guidance, ancestral wisdom, and primal energies are found. This mirrors Muladhara's role as the energetic gateway to survival wisdom and ancestral connection.

## Indigenous Perspectives
Indigenous peoples around the world emphasize **belonging to the land and to community** as the foundation of life. Many traditions teach that the earth is our Mother, and our survival depends on living in balance with her rhythms. In this view, to be ungrounded is not only an individual imbalance but also a disruption of harmony with tribe, ancestors, and the natural world. The Root Chakra echoes this truth: we are not separate from the soil that feeds us or the people who surround us.

## Earth-Based Spirituality
In earth-based practices such as Paganism, Wicca, and Druidry, the element of **Earth** represents stability, security, and the physical body. Rituals for grounding — standing barefoot on the ground, using stones, or visualizing roots growing from the feet — are central. The Root Chakra aligns with these practices as the energetic expression of our bond with Gaia, the living earth.

## A Shared Understanding
Whether through yogic philosophy, shamanic journeying, indigenous wisdom, or modern nature-based spirituality, the teaching is clear: **we are sustained by the earth, and our**

**survival depends on honoring that bond**. Muladhara is the chakra that reminds us of this timeless truth.

# Origins & Hidden History of Muladhara

The concept of Muladhara arises from the ancient yogic traditions of India, where the chakra system was first described in the **Tantras**. Texts such as the *Sat-Cakra-Nirupana* (circa 16th century) provide detailed imagery of the chakras, including the Root Chakra as a red, four-petaled lotus at the base of the spine. Within this lotus, the downward-pointing triangle symbolizes grounding energy and the pull of gravity, while the square represents stability and the unshakable foundation of life.

But the idea of a primal root — the **origin point of survival and support** — is not exclusive to yogic teachings. Traces of Root Chakra wisdom appear across cultures and centuries:

- **Vedic India**: Early Vedic hymns speak of *prana* (life force) flowing from the earth into the body, suggesting a foundational link between survival energy and the natural world.
- **Egyptian Mysteries**: Ancient Egypt emphasized the *Djed pillar*, symbolizing stability and endurance — qualities that echo the Root Chakra's essence.
- **Greek Philosophy**: The philosopher Empedocles taught of four elements, with **earth** as the grounding principle of matter and embodiment.
- **Chinese Medicine**: In Traditional Chinese Medicine, the **Kidney meridian** governs fear, vitality, and survival instincts, paralleling Muladhara's themes.
- **Kabbalistic Mysticism**: The sefirah *Malkuth*, meaning "Kingdom," represents the material world and physical foundation — a mirror of the root's function.

Over time, Muladhara became associated not only with survival but also with **spiritual potential**. Yogic adepts taught that Kundalini energy rests within this chakra, coiled like a serpent. To awaken higher consciousness, one must first awaken and stabilize the root — not to escape the body, but to transform it into a sacred vessel.

The "hidden history" of Muladhara lies in how societies have treated survival. In times of peace, grounding practices — farming, rituals of the land, ancestral remembrance — flourished. In times of upheaval, survival itself was threatened, and people were forced into fear, displacement, or disconnection from the earth. These collective wounds still echo in modern society as anxiety, scarcity mindsets, and ecological imbalance.

Understanding Muladhara's origins is more than learning its symbols. It is about remembering that survival has always been sacred. Food, shelter, tribe, and earth are not distractions from spiritual life — they are the **ground of being** from which all higher awareness rises.

# The Symbolism of the Root Chakra

Muladhara is associated with the **element of earth**, the densest and most stable of all the elements. Earth represents permanence, structure, and endurance — the qualities we rely on to survive and thrive. Just as the body cannot stand without bones, the spirit cannot ascend without the firm grounding of Muladhara.

Its **color is deep red**, the hue of primal vitality. Red is the color of blood, the life force that sustains us; of clay and soil, the substance that cradles our bodies and provides food; and of fire's embers, symbolizing survival energy in its most essential form. This red vibration connects us to instinct, alerting us to danger, energizing us in times of crisis, and reminding us of the preciousness of life.

## THE RED LOTUS

The lotus itself is always depicted as **deep red**, the color of blood, clay, and the life force of the physical body. Red symbolizes vitality, primal energy, and survival — the raw pulse of existence. Unlike the delicate pink lotus associated with higher chakras, the red lotus of Muladhara is dense, fertile, and elemental. It is not the flower of transcendence, but of embodiment.

## THE COLOR RED OF MULADHARA

When you close your eyes and visualize the Root Chakra, the color most often seen is **deep red.** This is not simply symbolic, but a vibrational truth that has been recognized across Tantric, yogic, and healing traditions. Red carries the resonance of earth energy, survival, and primal life force — the very essence of Muladhara.

## RED: SURVIVAL, VITALITY, AND GROUNDING

- **The Color of Life Force:** Red is the color of blood — the vital current flowing through every vein. It is the reminder that to live in a body is sacred. Each heartbeat pumps red life (blood) into every cell.
- **The Earth Beneath Our Feet:** Red is the color of soil and clay in many parts of the world. It represents the nourishment we receive from the land and the weight of belonging to the earth.
- **Instinct and Alertness:** Red stimulates awareness. It is the signal of danger and the fire of survival instinct. This intensity mirrors the Root's role in keeping us alert, safe, and prepared.
- **Strength and Endurance:** Red embodies the dense, heavy qualities of the Root Chakra — the energy that allows us to endure challenges and remain steady.

## WHY RED BELONGS TO THE ROOT

Each chakra color resonates with a specific frequency of light, forming the rainbow spectrum that mirrors the human energy system. Red, the lowest frequency and longest wavelength, grounds us in the material world.

- **The First Color of the Rainbow:** Red is always the base of the rainbow spectrum, just as Muladhara is the base of the chakra system.

- **The Slowest Vibration:** Its lower frequency resonates with the densest element — earth — anchoring us into gravity, body, and survival.
- **Rooted in Matter:** Red pulls energy downward and inward, reminding us that spirit cannot ascend without matter as its foundation.

## RED IN DAILY LIFE

- **When you feel scattered:** Wear red clothing or jewelry to bring awareness back to your body.
- **When you feel weak or drained:** Visualize breathing in red light, filling your bones and muscles with strength.
- **When you feel unsafe:** Place your bare feet on the ground and imagine red energy flowing from the earth into your Root Chakra.
- **In rituals of grounding:** Use red candles, red stones, or red fabrics to amplify the stabilizing qualities of Muladhara.

## MEDITATION WITH RED

1. Close your eyes and visualize a glowing red lotus at the base of your spine.
2. See the red light spreading down your legs, into your feet, and deep into the soil.
3. With every breath, imagine this red energy strengthening your foundation, reminding you: *"I am safe. I am grounded. I belong."*

## WANT TO EXPERIENCE IT IN ACTION?...
Watch this video for the Root Chakra Meditation.

Watch it here: https://youtu.be/NdNKIQWfjg0

## THE DEEPER LESSON OF RED

Red teaches us that survival is not separate from the sacred. To eat, to rest, to shelter, to stand firmly on the earth — these are spiritual acts when honored as divine. Just as a tree cannot rise without its roots, the soul cannot ascend without its grounding in red, earthy vitality.

The Root's red light is both a beginning and a constant companion. It is the steady flame that says: *"You are here. You are alive. You are safe."*

# The Four-Petaled Lotus of Muladhara

At the heart of Muladhara's symbolism lies a **red lotus with four petals**, one of the simplest yet most profound chakra images. Despite its simplicity compared to the intricate geometry of higher chakras, the four-petaled lotus carries immense meaning. It is a visual and energetic reminder that life begins with stability, order, and foundation.

### The Four Syllables

Each petal is inscribed with a Sanskrit seed sound: **vaṁ, śaṁ, ṣaṁ, and saṁ.** These bija syllables are not just letters but vibrations — the fundamental sounds that anchor consciousness into matter. Chanting or visualizing them aligns Muladhara with the vibrational blueprint of survival.

### The Four Qualities of Survival

The petals correspond to the most essential aspects of human life:

- **Stability** – the sense of being rooted and immovable, like the earth itself.

- **Security** – the assurance that one's basic needs can be met.
- **Instinct** – the primal awareness that ensures survival, the "fight, flight, or freeze" response when danger arises.
- **Basic Needs** – food, shelter, rest, and connection to community, without which life cannot be sustained.

Together, these petals form the energetic foundation of the entire chakra system. If one quality is missing, balance falters, just as a table collapses if even one leg is weak.

**The Four Directions**

The petals also reflect the **four directions — north, south, east, and west.** These represent the completeness of space, suggesting that Muladhara roots us not just in the body but in the very landscape of existence. When the Root is balanced, we feel at home in every direction, wherever life carries us.

**The Four Seasons**

In another interpretation, the four petals echo the **four seasons — spring, summer, autumn, winter.** Just as nature moves in cycles, Muladhara teaches us that survival depends on adaptability and trust in life's rhythms. Stability does not mean rigidity; it means flowing with change while remaining grounded.

**The Four Legs of the Table**

Perhaps the most practical symbol is that of a **four-legged table.** A table cannot stand on one, two, or three legs alone — it requires four for balance. Likewise, Muladhara needs all four qualities (stability, security, instinct, and basic needs) to support the weight of the human experience. This image reminds us that grounding is not a single practice but a holistic alignment of multiple aspects of survival.

**Balance and Steadiness**

Across these interpretations, the four-petaled lotus conveys one central truth: **without balance at the Root, nothing above can stand.** It is the square foundation beneath a temple, the soil beneath a tree, the bedrock of a mountain. The number four itself — associated with wholeness, order, and structure — reflects the unshakable steadiness that Muladhara embodies.

# The Triangle and the Square: Muladhara's Core Geometry

At the very heart of Muladhara's lotus rests a **downward-pointing triangle enclosed within a square.** These two geometric forms hold profound meaning, symbolizing the essential truths of incarnation and grounding.

**The Downward-Pointing Triangle**

- The downward triangle is the universal symbol of the **feminine, earth, and matter.** It channels energy downward, drawing spirit into form.
- In Tantric cosmology, it is the shape of **Shakti**, the divine feminine energy, that animates life. In Muladhara, this triangle represents Kundalini in her dormant state, coiled and waiting at the base of the spine.
- Its point facing down reminds us that enlightenment is not an escape upwards but a descent first into the body. To rise, we must first root.

- The triangle is also symbolic of **incarnation** — the descent of consciousness into flesh, the moment when spirit chooses to dwell in a physical body.

## The Square

- Surrounding the triangle is the **square**, the most stable of all shapes. With its equal sides and right angles, it represents foundation, order, and permanence.
- The square is the symbol of the **earth element (prithvi tattva)** — heavy, solid, unmoving. It grounds the dynamic energy of the triangle so that life can be sustained without chaos.
- Just as temples and sacred altars are traditionally built on a square base, the square in Muladhara signifies that spiritual ascent requires a stable earthly foundation.

## Union of Triangle and Square

Together, the triangle and square express a fundamental spiritual truth:

- The **triangle** reminds us of movement, flow, and descent into matter.

The **square** reminds us of structure, containment, and stability. When combined, they show that energy must be both **dynamic and anchored.** Too much movement without **grounding leads to instability; too much rigidity without flow leads to stagnation. Muladhara harmonizes both.**

## Returning to the Ground

While higher chakras lift energy upward into creativity, power, love, and transcendence, Muladhara's geometry points us back down. It teaches that no matter how high we climb into mystical states, we must eventually return to the body, to the earth, to the ground beneath us. Spirit and matter are not separate — they are two halves of the same truth, meeting in Muladhara.

This is the secret wisdom of the Root: **to be human is to live in both worlds at once — the infinite and the embodied, the eternal and the earthly.**

## THE TRIANGLE IN TAROT

- In esoteric Tarot traditions (Golden Dawn, Hermetic, and alchemical systems), the **triangle** is tied to the **elements**:
  - **Upward triangle:** Fire (will, transformation) and Air (thought, spirit).
  - **Downward triangle:** Water (emotion, receptivity) and Earth (matter, grounding).
- The **downward-pointing triangle** at Muladhara corresponds to the **element of Earth** in Tarot, grounding spirit into physical form.
- It also resonates with **The Empress (Major Arcana III)** — a card of fertility, earth, and embodiment — where divine creativity descends into matter.

## THE SQUARE IN TAROT

- The square is a symbol of **stability, order, and manifestation.** In Tarot, this appears in imagery like the **Throne of The Emperor (Major Arcana IV)** — the ruler of structure, foundation, and worldly security.
- In many Rider–Waite–Smith images, squares appear on garments (such as the checkered square design on The Magician's robe) or on thrones, symbolizing **control of the material plane.**
- The square is also linked to the **number 4 in numerology** (which governs Tarot's Fours), representing completion of a cycle, grounding, and security:

- o *Four of Pentacles* — holding tightly to material stability.
- o *Four of Wands* — the stability of home, community, and celebration.
- o *Four of Swords* — rest and recovery within structure.
- o *Four of Cups* — emotional grounding or stagnation.

## TRIANGLE + SQUARE TOGETHER

When the **triangle and square unite** in Muladhara's symbol, they mirror Tarot's interplay between **dynamic energy (triangle)** and **fixed foundation (square).**

- The triangle brings movement (spirit descending into matter).
- The square provides containment (order, stability, survival).

This duality echoes:

- **The Magician (I):** Channeling divine energy downward into physical manifestation (as above, so below).
- **The World (XXI):** Surrounded by the four corners (tetramorph of fixed zodiac signs, representing stability) yet containing movement and flow within.

## ROOT CHAKRA RESONANCE IN TAROT

- The Root Chakra's earth-bound geometry resonates most strongly with the **Suit of Pentacles**, which governs material survival, security, and embodiment.
- It also resonates with the **number 4** cards and Major Arcana figures who embody structure and grounding (The Emperor, The World).

Muladhara is both **the beginning and the support of the journey.** It is the first chakra to form in early childhood, carrying the memory of safety or instability into all later experiences. It is also the ever-present foundation that holds us steady no matter how high we climb in consciousness. Without Muladhara, the entire chakra system is unrooted, like a tree without soil. With it, we gain the strength to stand tall, endure hardship, and rise toward spiritual awakening with confidence.

In this way, Muladhara is not simply a starting point — it is a **constant companion**. Every step we take in healing, every moment of spiritual growth, is supported by this chakra. As we expand upward toward vision and transcendence, Muladhara keeps us rooted, reminding us that enlightenment is not escape but embodiment.

# Muladhara In Yogic Practice

In the earliest Tantric and yogic traditions, the chakras were not described as physical organs, but as **focal points for meditation and spiritual awakening.** Yogis would concentrate on each chakra through a combination of visualization, breath, mantra, and subtle awareness, activating deeper layers of consciousness.

For **Muladhara,** the Root Chakra, the practice centered on stability, survival, and grounding into the body. The bija mantra, or "seed sound," of Muladhara is **LAM** — a vibrational key said to anchor energy downward and awaken the earth element within. Meditating on the four-petaled lotus and chanting "LAM" connected practitioners directly to the qualities of safety, stability, and belonging.

The goal was not only physical health but also **spiritual embodiment.** While higher chakras opened perception and transcendence, Muladhara established the secure foundation for those awakenings. Yogis recognized that without a stable Root, the ascent of kundalini and the flowering of higher consciousness could not occur safely or sustainably.

## THE INNER SYMBOL OF MULADHARA

At the very center of Muladhara's image, inside the square and downward-pointing triangle, is the Sanskrit syllable **LAM (लं)**. This bija mantra is more than a sound; it is the vibrational essence of grounding, the resonance that links body and spirit to the earth.

## WHAT LAM REPRESENTS

- **Vibrational Key:** LAM is the sound that "unlocks" the Root Chakra, harmonizing the body with stability, security, and survival instincts.
- **Sound of the Earth:** When chanted, LAM vibrates through the pelvis, hips, and legs — physically activating the energetic foundation of the human system.
- **Dissolver of Fear:** Ancient texts describe LAM as a stabilizer against fear, anxiety, and instability, helping dissolve the survival stress that contracts the Root.
- **Link to Earth Element:** Each chakra aligns with an element; Muladhara is tied to **earth (prithvi).** LAM harmonizes the body with gravity, solidity, and the nourishing stability of the ground beneath us.

Through the practice of meditating on Muladhara's lotus and chanting LAM, yogis learned to embody both the **instinctual wisdom of survival** and the **sacredness of incarnation.** The Root was not seen as lower or lesser, but as the fertile soil from which all spiritual growth arises.

# The Seed Sound of Muladhara: LAM

At the very center of the Root Chakra's symbol lies not just form and geometry, but sound. In Tantric teachings, every chakra has a **bija mantra** — a "seed sound" said to contain the vibrational essence of that energy center. For Muladhara, the Root Chakra, the bija is **LAM** (pronounced "Lahm," like "lawn" with an "m").

## WHY SOUND MATTERS

In the Sanskrit tradition, **sound is creation.** It is vibration, frequency, and energy condensed into audible form. The universe itself, according to yogic philosophy, began with the primal sound *OM.* In the same way, each chakra has a specific vibrational "key" that unlocks its energy field.

For Muladhara, that sound is **LAM.** Chanting it is like striking the exact note that anchors consciousness into the body and grounds scattered energy into stability.

## THE POWER OF LAM

- **Resonance in the Lower Body:** When chanted, LAM naturally vibrates through the pelvis, hips, and legs, stimulating the Root and its connection to the earth.
- **Releasing Fear:** Fear unsettles the Root, pulling us into survival stress. LAM soothes that vibration, restoring safety and calm.
- **Grounding Energy:** LAM draws prana downward, anchoring higher thoughts and emotions into physical form.
- **Reconnecting with Earth:** The sound reminds the body of its deep belonging to nature, to soil, and to the cycles of life.

## HOW TO CHANT LAM

### Step 1 – Prepare the Body

- Sit cross-legged or with feet flat on the floor.
- Place your hands on your knees or over your lower belly.
- Take 3–5 slow breaths, feeling the weight of your body resting on the ground.

### Step 2 – Focus on the Root

- Visualize a glowing red lotus at the base of your spine.
- See it pulsing with life energy, connected by roots deep into the earth.

### Step 3 – Chant the Sound

- Inhale deeply. As you exhale, chant: **LAAAAHHHHMmmmm…**
- Allow the "Lah" to resonate in the open mouth, then let the "mmm" hum through the pelvis and down the legs.
- Feel the vibration anchoring you firmly into the ground.

### Step 4 – Repeat Rhythmically

- Chant LAM 7, 12, or 108 times.
- With each repetition, imagine the red lotus petals unfolding, radiating stability and strength.

### Step 5 – Silent Resonance

- After chanting, sit quietly. Listen inwardly. Feel the echo of LAM vibrating in your bones, like the steady hum of the earth itself.

## WAYS TO USE LAM IN PRACTICE

- **Morning Grounding:** Chant LAM three times upon waking to anchor your day in stability.
- **Stress Release:** When feeling anxious or scattered, chant LAM until your breath deepens and your body relaxes.
- **Healing Sessions:** Practitioners may chant LAM silently while working near the feet, legs, or hips to enhance grounding.
- **Movement Integration:** Combine chanting with gentle stomping, walking barefoot, or yoga poses like Mountain and Warrior.
- **Group Practice:** Chanting LAM together magnifies the grounding effect, creating a collective field of stability and safety.

## ROOT-CENTERED AFFIRMATION WITH LAM

*"As I chant LAM, I root deeply. I am safe. I am grounded. I belong to the earth and the earth belongs to me."*

# The Animal Symbol Of Muladhara: The Elephant

In the ancient chakra system, each energy center was given an animal guide — a living emblem that embodied its essence in form. For the Root Chakra, that animal is the **elephant**, often depicted with **seven trunks**, symbolizing its immense power and multidimensional grounding.

## WHY THE ELEPHANT?

The elephant is one of the most revered creatures in both yogic and cultural traditions, known for its **strength, wisdom, and**

**endurance.** Its massive body and steady gait embody the immovable presence of earth itself. Just as an elephant stands firm, unshaken by storms, Muladhara provides the resilience to withstand life's challenges.

- **Strength and Power:** With its size and weight, the elephant is the very image of stability. This reflects the Root Chakra's ability to anchor us in our body and environment.
- **Endurance:** Elephants walk great distances, carrying heavy loads, yet they do so with patience and persistence. Likewise, Muladhara supports our long journey through life.
- **Wisdom and Memory:** Known for their extraordinary memory, elephants remind us that survival is not only physical but also rooted in ancestral knowledge. Muladhara carries these deep imprints, including generational lessons and karmic patterns.
- **Protection:** Elephants protect their herd with fierce loyalty. A balanced Root fosters the same protective instinct — toward self, family, and community.

## SYMBOLISM OF THE SEVEN TRUNKS

In Tantric depictions, the elephant of Muladhara is shown with **seven trunks.** Each trunk can be seen as a channel of grounding power, drawing from the seven layers of existence (physical, energetic, emotional, mental, ancestral, karmic, and spiritual). It also echoes the seven chakras themselves, suggesting that every higher energy center depends on the Root for stability.

## SYMBOLISM IN THE ROOT CHAKRA

The elephant represents:

- **Stability:** Firm-footed and immovable, like the solid earth beneath us.

- **Ancestral Strength:** The wisdom carried in bones, blood, and memory.
- **Community:** Elephants live in herds, mirroring our need for connection and belonging.
- **Sacred Grounding:** The elephant is associated with Lord Ganesha in Hindu tradition, the remover of obstacles, who blesses beginnings and ensures steady foundations.

## MEDITATING WITH THE ELEPHANT

- **Visualization:** Imagine a great red elephant standing at the base of your spine. With each breath, feel its weight pressing into the earth, its trunks rooting you deeper into safety.
- **Affirmation:** *"I am strong. I am steady. I am rooted in wisdom and earth."*
- **Nature Practice:** Observe the qualities of grounded animals — their calmness, patience, and endurance. Let those qualities infuse your own presence.

## THE DEEPER LESSON

The elephant shows us that the Root is not about fragility, but about **immovable presence.** Fear may shake us, life may challenge us, but a balanced Muladhara allows us to endure with dignity and strength. Just as an elephant never forgets, the Root carries both the burdens and the blessings of our lineage. By healing it, we release fear and reclaim ancestral resilience.

The elephant, steady and wise, reminds us that **true power does not rush or force — it simply *is*.**

# The Deities Of The Root Chakra

In Tantric tradition, each chakra is presided over by deities who embody its essential qualities. These figures are not just external gods to be worshipped — they are inner archetypes, reflections of energies within us that can be awakened through meditation and practice.

For **Muladhara**, the Root Chakra, the presiding deities express the themes of **stability, protection, survival, and the grounding of spirit into matter.**

## BRAHMA – THE CREATOR AND SUSTAINER OF FOUNDATIONS

- **Brahma**, the four-headed creator god, is often associated with Muladhara as its presiding deity.
- As the force of creation, Brahma symbolizes the grounding of spirit into the physical world — the moment consciousness takes form.
- In the Root, he represents the enduring power of beginnings, the strength of foundations, and the sacredness of survival.
- Meditating on Brahma within Muladhara connects us to the creative impulse of life itself: the choice to exist, to root, and to endure.

## DAKINI – THE FEMININE GUARDIAN OF MULADHARA

- The Shakti energy of the Root is often personified as **Dakini**, a goddess of raw, grounding power.
- She is portrayed with red or earthy energy, holding symbols of strength and protection.
- Dakini embodies primal survival wisdom — instinct, stability, and the fierce guardianship of life.

- As the awakened feminine of Muladhara, she helps us reclaim safety in our bodies and trust in the earth beneath us.

TOGETHER: BRAHMA AND DAKINI

Together, Brahma and Dakini balance the Root's dual nature:

- **Brahma** provides order, structure, and the foundation of creation.
- **Dakini** provides the life-force energy, the Shakti that animates and protects that creation.

Their union reminds us that grounding is not passive; it is both **structure and energy, form and vitality.** To root ourselves is to unite these forces within.

# Root Deities in Other Traditions

Though Tantra specifically names Brahma and Dakini, many traditions personify the qualities of the Root through sacred figures:

- In Hindu culture, **Ganesha**, the elephant-headed god, is also connected to Muladhara — as the remover of obstacles, guardian of beginnings, and deity of grounding.
- In Indigenous cosmologies, the **Earth Mother** is the primordial Root deity, holding all beings in her body and providing food, shelter, and life.
- In Western mysticism, the Root finds resonance in the **Archangel Uriel** — "Light of God" — who governs the earth element, protection, and stability.

These parallels reveal a universal recognition: across cultures, the Root is guarded by deities of **earth, beginnings, and protection.**

# The Element Of Muladhara: Earth (Prithvi)

Each chakra is traditionally aligned with one of the five great elements of nature (*pancha mahabhutas*). For the Root Chakra, that element is **earth — Prithvi in Sanskrit.** This is not a symbolic guesswork; it is a direct reflection of Muladhara's qualities: stability, survival, and foundation.

## EARTH AS THE GROUND OF BEING

Earth is solid. It carries weight, form, and durability. It is the soil beneath our feet, the body that holds us upright, the stone mountains that endure for millennia. Just as the Root Chakra is our foundation in the chakra system, earth is the foundation of life itself.

- **Weight and Stability:** Earth pulls us down through gravity, reminding us we belong here. When Muladhara is strong, we feel steady, immovable, and grounded.
- **Nourishment and Support:** Just as soil nourishes a seed into a tree, the earth provides the food, shelter, and resources that sustain human life. Muladhara teaches us to receive this support with gratitude.
- **Cycles and Seasons:** Earth holds the memory of time — spring's renewal, summer's growth, autumn's harvest, and winter's rest. The Root Chakra connects us to these cycles of survival and regeneration.

## WHY EARTH BELONGS TO THE ROOT

The chakras ascend through the elements: earth (root), water (sacral), fire (solar plexus), air (heart), and ether/space (throat), moving toward subtler energies. Earth is the heaviest and most solid, making it the natural anchor. It is the beginning, the ground zero of embodiment.

Muladhara asks us to:

- **Anchor rather than drift.**
- **Stabilize rather than scatter.**
- **Build foundations rather than leap ahead.**

Earth is the element of incarnation — the commitment to live fully in a body, on this planet, in this moment.

## MEDITATING ON EARTH

Bringing the element of earth into Root Chakra practices is both simple and profound:

1. **Body Scan Meditation:** Lie flat on the ground. Feel every part of your body sinking into the earth. Whisper silently: *"I am held. I am safe."*
2. **Stone or Crystal Practice:** Hold a stone (hematite, jasper, or simply a river rock). Feel its weight. Breathe with it as a reminder of your own solidity.
3. **Visualization:** Imagine a glowing red square at the base of your spine. From it, roots extend deep into the soil, wrapping around stones and roots below, anchoring you to the earth's heart.

## EARTH IN DAILY LIFE

- **When you feel scattered:** Cook and eat root vegetables slowly. Let the act of nourishment ground you.
- **When anxiety arises:** Press your feet firmly into the floor, imagining roots digging into the ground beneath.
- **When you feel disconnected from your body:** Take a barefoot walk on soil, sand, or grass. Reconnect through touch.
- **When life feels unstable:** Simplify. Clear clutter. Return to routines and foundations.

## THE LESSON OF EARTH

Earth reminds us that true strength comes from stability, not from speed. Just as a tree cannot grow without roots, we cannot reach spiritual heights without grounding. Muladhara teaches us that **safety, survival, and foundation are not limitations — they are the sacred soil in which all growth begins.**

A Root aligned with earth becomes a mountain: steady, enduring, and unshakable.

## BRINGING THE SYMBOLS TOGETHER

Taken together, these symbols form a complete picture of the Root Chakra's role:

- The lotus petals reflect the primal energies of survival and stability.
- The square grounds us in the element of earth.
- The downward triangle directs energy into embodiment.
- The elephant offers strength and endurance.

To meditate on these symbols is to invite their qualities into your own life. Each image is a reminder that grounding is not passive — it is a living relationship with the earth, the body, and the instincts that sustain life.

# The Root As The Sacred Cavern

Long before chakras were drawn as colored wheels or lotuses, the sages described the **Muladhara** as a hidden cavern deep within the body. It was imagined not as an airy space, but as an **earth chamber** — a root cellar of the soul — where the first spark of life energy resides.

### THE CAVERN BELOW

While the heart was seen as a luminous cave within, the Root was envisioned as a **subterranean sanctum** — the inner ground that lies beneath all layers of awareness. Yogis taught that if you follow your awareness downward in meditation, past the shifting thoughts and emotions, you arrive at this cavern.

Here, resting at the base of the spine, lies the **coiled serpent of Kundalini**, silent and dormant, awaiting awakening. This cavern is not empty — it is dense, fertile, vibrating with potential energy. It is the womb of both survival and transcendence.

### WHY THE ROOT?

The Root is the seat of incarnation, the tether between soul and soil. To enter its cavern is to touch the most primal truth: *you are here, embodied, alive.*

- **In Tantra:** Muladhara is the storehouse of Shakti, the latent power that fuels all transformation.
- **In Yoga:** It is the "foundation place," the first support, without which higher states cannot endure.

- **In Indigenous Mysticism:** Caves and earth chambers are sacred womb-spaces — entrances to the underworld, the ancestors, and the Mother's body.

Across cultures, the Root has always been linked to the **earth below** — to caves, mountains, wombs, and the dark, fertile spaces where life begins.

## THE ROOT CHAKRA AS A MAP

The Root Chakra's lotus — with its four petals, square, and downward-pointing triangle — can be seen as a symbolic map into this cavern. The petals are the directions; the square is the threshold of matter; the triangle is the descent. Together, they guide awareness down into the subterranean chamber where Kundalini rests, holding the memory of survival and the seed of awakening.

## A PRACTICE: ENTERING THE CAVERN

1. Close your eyes. Place your hands on your lower belly or base of your spine.
2. Imagine a doorway in the earth beneath you, opening gently.
3. Step inward in your mind's eye, descending into a hidden cavern.
4. At the center, see a coiled serpent or glowing ember — silent, powerful, eternal.
5. Sit before this energy with respect. Know that it is your foundation, your hidden root, your inner source of power.

## THE DEEPER LESSON

The cavern of the Root reminds us that spirituality does not float above life — it **roots into the ground of being.** The world may be unstable, the mind restless, the emotions overwhelming

— but beneath it all, there is a cavern inside you that is unshaken.

To return to this cavern is to return to stability.
To live from this cavern is to live anchored, strong, and unafraid.

## THE WESTERN ADAPTATION

When the chakra system was introduced to the West in the late 19th and early 20th centuries, much of its original cultural and spiritual context was reshaped. Theosophists such as **C.W. Leadbeater** and **Alice Bailey** translated chakra teachings into terms that Western audiences could understand, emphasizing their connection to health, psychology, and spiritual evolution rather than strictly yogic meditation.

In this adaptation, the **Root Chakra** was reinterpreted as the foundation of the human energy system, symbolizing survival, grounding, and security. This framing aligned with Western psychology, which often looked at human development through the lens of basic needs. Later, **Carl Jung** drew parallels between Muladhara and the earliest stages of **individuation**, suggesting that before one can evolve spiritually, one must establish stability, safety, and a sense of belonging.

By the mid-20th century, as the New Age movement blossomed, healers and energy workers expanded these ideas further. The Root Chakra became associated with issues of **fear, stability, money, home, and physical health.** While ancient yogis focused on Muladhara as the seat of Kundalini Shakti and the anchor of embodiment, Western teachers often emphasized its role in practical living — balancing emotions, overcoming insecurity, and building a stable foundation for growth.

Today, in Western Reiki, yoga, and energy healing traditions, the Root Chakra is frequently taught as the key to **feeling safe**

**in the body, connected to the earth, and supported by life itself.** Though this perspective sometimes simplifies the deeper esoteric symbolism, it remains true to the essence of Muladhara: without grounding, no healing or spiritual ascent can last.

The hidden history of the Root shows us that this chakra is not a modern invention — it belongs to an ancient lineage of wisdom stretching back thousands of years. As we continue in this book, we will draw upon both its **original yogic roots** and its **modern applications**, weaving together a fuller, richer understanding of Muladhara's energy in our lives today.

# Archetypes of the Root Chakra

Every chakra expresses itself through patterns of thought, feeling, and behavior. These patterns often crystallize into **archetypes** — universal roles or identities that reveal both the light and shadow sides of an energy center. For the Root Chakra, two archetypes stand out: **The Survivor** and **The Provider**.

**The Survivor**

The Survivor represents the most primal aspect of Muladhara: the instinct to stay alive. This archetype embodies resilience, resourcefulness, and determination. The Survivor finds ways to endure even in the harshest circumstances, teaching us that within each of us lies an unbreakable will to live.

- **In Balance**: The Survivor archetype brings courage, adaptability, and perseverance. It knows that life is worth fighting for and draws strength from the earth itself. People expressing this archetype in balance can navigate uncertainty with trust that their needs will be met.

- **In Shadow**: When distorted, the Survivor can manifest as chronic fear, hypervigilance, or a scarcity mindset. Instead of feeling grounded, life becomes a constant battle, as if danger is always around the corner. This creates anxiety, distrust, and difficulty resting in the present.

The Survivor teaches us that safety is not just physical but also psychological — the inner knowing that we can endure and thrive, even when circumstances challenge us.

## The Provider

Where the Survivor is focused on enduring, the Provider ensures that survival becomes sustainable. This archetype is connected to tribe, family, and community. It seeks to create shelter, food, stability, and protection not only for oneself but also for others.

- **In Balance**: The Provider is nurturing, dependable, and generous. It establishes secure homes, creates strong community bonds, and ensures that basic needs are met. People embodying this archetype in balance carry a quiet strength that others can lean on.
- **In Shadow**: When unbalanced, the Provider may slip into over-responsibility, control, or fear of losing stability. It may hoard resources, cling to possessions, or create rigid routines in an attempt to guarantee safety. Instead of offering support, the shadow Provider becomes weighed down by the burden of always holding everything together.

The Provider reminds us that survival is not only individual — it is collective. Our sense of safety deepens when we are cared for, and when we, in turn, provide stability to those around us.

**Living Archetypally**

Both the Survivor and the Provider live within us. Sometimes one voice is louder than the other, depending on our history and present circumstances. By recognizing these archetypes, we can see where we are rooted in strength and where fear may be distorting our foundation.

Living archetypally with Muladhara means balancing the Survivor's resilience with the Provider's nurturing presence. Together, they remind us that to feel safe in the world is both to endure and to belong.

# Root Archetype Reflection Exercise

The archetypes of the Root Chakra — **The Survivor** and **The Provider** — live in all of us. Sometimes they guide us toward balance and resilience; other times they reveal our fears and imbalances. Reflection helps us recognize where these archetypes show up in our lives and how we can align them with stability and trust.

Take a few quiet moments for this exercise. Find a comfortable position with your feet firmly on the ground. Close your eyes, take three deep breaths, and imagine roots growing downward from your body into the earth. As you feel grounded, reflect on the questions below. Write your responses in a journal, allowing honesty and insight to flow freely.

**Exploring the Survivor**

1. When have I relied on my inner Survivor to overcome difficulty?
2. How do I respond to uncertainty or crisis — with trust, or with fear?
3. What strengths does my Survivor archetype bring me?

4. In what ways might my Survivor slip into shadow — fear of scarcity, hypervigilance, or constant worry?
5. What grounding practice helps my Survivor feel safe enough to rest?

## Exploring the Provider

1. When do I feel most like a Provider — caring for others, offering stability, or creating a safe space?
2. How do I balance my responsibility to others with caring for myself?
3. In what ways do I provide security, resources, or belonging for my family, friends, or community?
4. Where might my Provider archetype become unbalanced — taking on too much, trying to control, or hoarding resources?
5. What would it feel like to trust that I am enough, and that I provide enough?

## Integration

- Which archetype feels stronger in me right now — Survivor or Provider?
- Where do I notice shadow patterns in either archetype?
- What small step can I take this week to bring my Root energy into greater balance?

## Reflection Mantra:

*"I honor the Survivor within me for keeping me alive. I honor the Provider within me for creating safety. Together they root me in trust, stability, and belonging."*

# Chapter 3 – The Energetic Blueprint of the Root

## The Root Chakra and the Aura

The Root Chakra does more than keep us physically alive — it establishes the **energetic foundation of the aura**, the subtle field of light and vibration that surrounds the body. Just as a building requires a strong foundation to support its walls and roof, the aura depends on Muladhara's stability to hold its shape and integrity.

When Muladhara is strong, the aura is **dense, grounded, and resilient**. It feels like a protective shield that keeps you steady in chaotic environments. You may notice that you "hold your space" more easily, that negative energy rolls off you, and that you recover quickly after stress. The aura radiates a deep red hue near the base of the body, gradually blending with the other colors of the chakra system as it moves upward.

When Muladhara is weak or blocked, the aura can appear **thin, fragmented, or porous**. This makes you feel vulnerable to outside influences, easily drained, or disconnected from your own body. People with imbalances at the root often describe themselves as "ungrounded" — a sensation of being scattered, unprotected, or not fully "in" their body.

The Root Chakra anchors the aura to the earth itself. This is why grounding practices — standing barefoot on the soil, visualizing roots extending downward, or simply breathing deeply into the lower body — can instantly strengthen the energy field. These practices send a signal to Muladhara: *I am here. I am safe. I belong.* In response, the aura expands, stabilizes, and becomes more luminous.

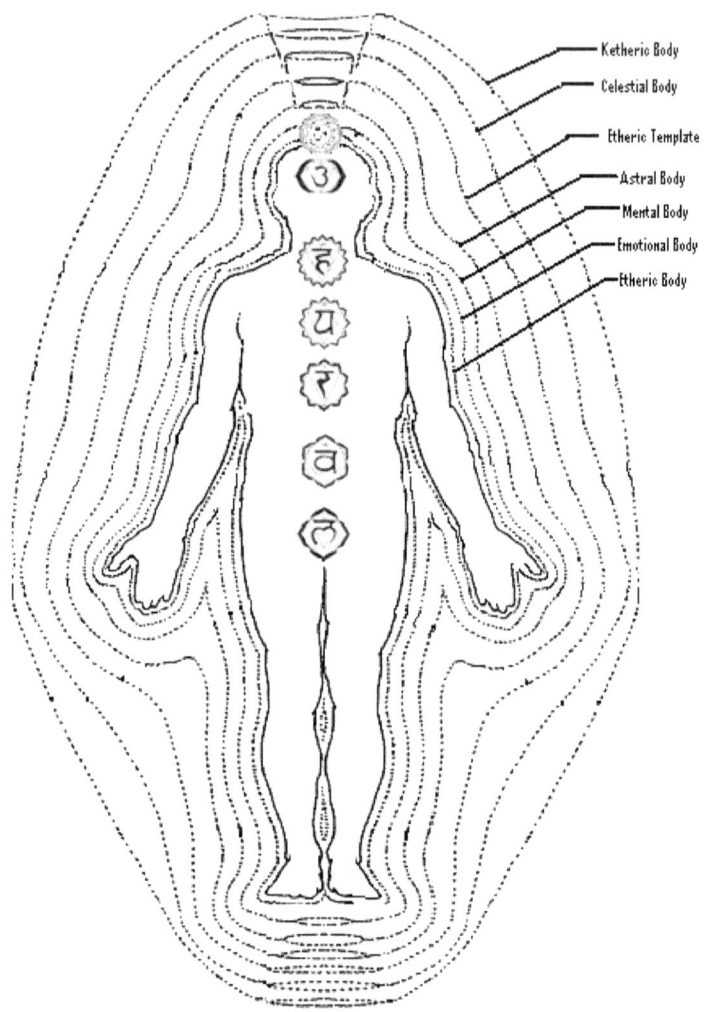

From a practitioner's perspective, the Root Chakra is often the first place to check when someone's aura feels unstable. Even if the upper chakras appear bright, without grounding in Muladhara the aura lacks cohesion. Like a tree without roots, it may appear lush but can be toppled by the slightest storm.

In this way, Muladhara serves as the **energetic blueprint for the aura** — the invisible structure that determines whether our energy field can hold, heal, and protect us.

# Flow of Energy from the Root Upward

The Root Chakra is not an isolated energy center — it is the **gateway through which life force enters the body and begins its ascent through the chakra system**. In yogic tradition, this life force is called **prana**, and in the Tantric teachings, the dormant serpent energy of **Kundalini** rests coiled at the base of the spine in Muladhara, waiting for the right conditions to awaken and rise.

Energy at the Root begins with the most essential aspects of life: survival, stability, and belonging. Once these are secured, the energy naturally rises to higher expressions:

- From **Muladhara (Root)** → to **Svadhisthana (Sacral)**, survival energy evolves into creativity, pleasure, and the flow of emotions.
- From **Sacral** → to **Manipura (Solar Plexus)**, creativity gains direction and transforms into power, confidence, and will.
- From **Manipura** → to **Anahata (Heart)**, power softens into compassion, connection, and love.
- And so the energy continues upward, toward truth, vision, and transcendence.

This **ascending flow** reflects a universal law: life begins at the foundation and moves upward toward expansion. A child must learn to walk before running, to speak before expressing vision, to feel safe before exploring love. Likewise, energy must be rooted before it can rise.

When Muladhara is balanced, this upward flow is steady and harmonious. Each chakra receives what it needs to blossom. But when the Root is weak, blocked, or unstable, the entire system above it struggles. Emotional swings, lack of confidence, or even spiritual disconnection can often be traced back to a shaky foundation at the Root.

Practitioners often describe this as a **current of energy** that rises through the central channel of the body, the *sushumna nadi*. The Root provides the pressure, like water flowing from an underground spring. If the spring is blocked, the stream dries up; if it is overflowing chaotically, the higher chakras may be overwhelmed.

A balanced Root Chakra does not "trap" energy at the bottom. Instead, it **grounds the flow so it can rise safely**. Like the roots of a tree, Muladhara ensures that energy drawn from the earth nourishes the entire system — trunk, branches, leaves, and blossoms.

# The Root as the Seat of Instinct and Survival

If the heart is the seat of love, then the root is the seat of **instinct**. Muladhara governs the primal intelligence that keeps us alive — the part of us that reacts before thought, that knows when to run, rest, or reach for nourishment. This survival wisdom is not intellectual; it is cellular, woven into the very fabric of the body.

From an evolutionary perspective, Muladhara reflects the earliest layers of human development. Long before philosophy, art, or spiritual practice, our ancestors needed to secure food, shelter, and safety. Their lives depended on the very qualities the Root Chakra embodies: strength, resilience, endurance, and the ability to adapt to changing conditions. These instincts are still alive within us today, and they surface whenever survival feels threatened.

When the Root Chakra is in balance, instincts act as trustworthy guides. You may feel a "gut sense" of when to take action, when to wait, or when to walk away. You experience an underlying confidence that life supports you, even when uncertainty arises. This balanced instinct creates **calm resilience** — the ability to move forward without panic, trusting the ground beneath your feet.

When Muladhara is out of balance, instincts can become distorted. Fear may override intuition, causing hypervigilance, anxiety, or the sense of being constantly unsafe. Or instincts may be dulled, leaving a person disconnected from their body's signals, unable to recognize hunger, fatigue, or danger until imbalance becomes extreme. In both cases, survival energy is present but misdirected.

Muladhara also governs the **fight-flight-freeze response**, mediated by the adrenal glands and nervous system. This ancient mechanism is meant to protect us in moments of true threat, but in modern life, it is often overstimulated. Chronic stress, societal instability, and unresolved trauma keep the root locked in survival mode. Instead of being a supportive base, it becomes a source of constant alarm.

Healing the Root Chakra restores instinct to its natural place: a **compass, not a prison**. When instincts are trusted and balanced, they help us live with presence, vitality, and security. We can move beyond mere survival into thriving — not abandoning our roots, but allowing them to sustain us while we reach for higher growth.

# A Universal Understanding of Grounding

Though chakras originate in the yogic traditions of India, the experience of **grounding** is universal. Across cultures, times, and languages, human beings have understood the need to connect with the earth as the basis of strength, safety, and balance.

To be grounded is to feel **present, steady, and connected** — to yourself, to your body, and to the world around you. It is that deep sense of "I am here, I belong, I am supported." Whether through ritual, prayer, or daily habit, grounding practices arise naturally in every culture because the human spirit instinctively seeks stability before expansion.

- **Indigenous traditions** teach grounding through walking barefoot on the earth, honoring the land, and recognizing the body as part of the natural world.
- **Shamanic practices** often begin by calling in the four directions and connecting to the "lower world," a realm symbolizing the fertile foundation beneath.
- **Eastern systems** like yoga and Taoism emphasize rooting energy downward before lifting it upward, teaching that flow must begin with a stable base.
- **Western mysticism** uses images like the Tree of Life or the stone foundation of a temple to remind us that spirit is sustained by matter.

Even in **modern psychology**, grounding is recognized as a vital tool for wellbeing. Therapists use grounding techniques — breathing, sensory awareness, touch, movement — to help people regulate emotions, reduce anxiety, and return to the present moment.

What all these perspectives share is the recognition that grounding is not merely physical. It is **energetic and spiritual**.

We may eat nourishing food and stand on solid ground, but if we feel unsafe, disconnected, or rootless inside, no external structure can provide lasting security. True grounding arises when body, mind, and spirit all affirm: *I am safe. I am here. Life supports me.*

In this way, grounding is both **universal and personal**. It is as simple as feeling your feet on the earth, yet as profound as realizing that your existence is part of something vast and interconnected. Muladhara holds this truth: grounding is not a chore or limitation — it is the gift of being alive, embodied, and rooted in the living earth.

# How Practitioners Work with the Root Chakra

For healers and energy practitioners, the Root Chakra is often the **first point of assessment** in any session. Even when a client comes with issues in the heart, mind, or spirit, practitioners know that instability at Muladhara can ripple upward and affect the entire energetic system.

**Assessment**
Practitioners may begin by observing whether a client feels grounded — are their feet firmly on the floor, is their breathing shallow or deep, do they seem present in their body? Questions about safety, stability, family history, and stress levels often reveal whether the Root Chakra is balanced or imbalanced. Energy-sensitive practitioners may also notice the aura around the base of the spine, hips, and legs — appearing either solid and vibrant or weak and fragmented.

## Energy Healing Techniques

- **Reiki & Hands-On Healing**: Practitioners often place their hands over the lower spine, hips, knees, or feet, channeling energy to strengthen the base.
- **Sound Healing**: Drumming, low-toned chanting, or playing instruments that emphasize deep resonance (such as didgeridoo or bass singing bowls) help stabilize the Root. The *LAM* mantra is frequently used in toning practices.
- **Crystal Healing**: Stones like hematite, red jasper, garnet, smoky quartz, and black tourmaline are placed on or near the Root Chakra, or even beneath the feet, to anchor and stabilize energy.
- **Aromatherapy**: Essential oils such as vetiver, cedarwood, patchouli, and sandalwood are used to promote a sense of safety and grounding.

## Bodywork Practices

Many practitioners integrate physical techniques to awaken Root energy. Massage, reflexology of the feet, and somatic exercises that emphasize rooting into the legs and hips can restore flow at Muladhara. Movement practices like yoga asanas (mountain pose, warrior poses, or squats) are often recommended to reinforce grounding both during and after a session.

## Spiritual and Ancestral Work

Some practitioners focus on clearing ancestral fear or survival trauma held in the Root Chakra. Guided meditation, shamanic journeying, or cord-releasing techniques are used to address inherited patterns of insecurity, scarcity, or displacement. By working through these root-level memories, the client begins to reclaim safety not only for themselves but for generations past and future.

**Integration**

Ultimately, practitioners remind clients that healing the Root is about more than temporary relief. It requires ongoing grounding rituals — daily practices that reaffirm safety, connection, and stability. Whether through breath, movement, nature, or ritual, the Root must be tended to consistently, like the soil that nourishes a growing tree.

For healers, Muladhara is both a starting place and a constant anchor. It teaches that no matter how high consciousness climbs, the work is incomplete unless it is rooted in the ground of being.

# Chapter 4 – Signs of Imbalance

## Shadow Aspects of the Root Chakra

Every chakra has both its gifts and its shadows. While the Root Chakra offers stability, security, and grounding, its shadow aspects emerge when survival energy becomes distorted. These shadows are not "bad" in themselves — they are signals, showing us where safety has been compromised or fear has taken root.

The Root's shadow is often tied to **fear, insecurity, and survival instincts gone awry**. Instead of serving as a foundation of trust, Muladhara may become a well of anxiety, scarcity, or hypervigilance. These shadows can manifest physically, emotionally, and spiritually.

**Fear and Anxiety**

The most common shadow of the Root is fear. When Muladhara is unstable, fear arises not only in times of real danger but as a constant undercurrent in daily life. This may feel like chronic anxiety, restlessness, or a sense of being unsafe in the world. Fear narrows the aura, making it harder to feel expansive, joyful, or connected.

**Scarcity and Survival Mindset**

Another shadow of the Root is scarcity — the belief that there is never enough: not enough money, food, time, or security. This mindset drives hoarding, overworking, or clinging to possessions as a substitute for safety. Instead of grounding us, the Root becomes a prison of "not enough," keeping us in survival mode long after the danger has passed.

### Disconnection from the Body

When Muladhara is wounded, we may feel disembodied or disconnected from the physical self. Symptoms include difficulty being present, a tendency to live in the mind, or ignoring the body's signals of hunger, fatigue, or pain. Spiritually, this can manifest as trying to "escape upward" into higher chakras without tending to the root.

### Instability and Restlessness

Imbalance in the Root often creates instability — difficulty maintaining a job, a home, or consistent routines. A person may move from place to place, relationship to relationship, or idea to idea without feeling grounded. Life feels chaotic, like trying to build a house on shifting sand.

### Aggression and Over-Control

Sometimes the Root's shadow swings the other way — instead of too little grounding, there is too much. This can appear as rigidity, stubbornness, greed, or aggression. Control becomes the false substitute for true security. People in this state may cling to power, possessions, or routines, fearing collapse if they let go.

# Blocked or Deficient Root Energy

When the Root Chakra is **blocked or underactive**, the flow of life force energy becomes weak or fragmented. Instead of feeling safe and grounded, a person may experience disconnection, insecurity, and chronic instability. The body and mind struggle to find a firm foundation, leading to survival fears that linger even when physical needs are met.

## Fear

Fear is the clearest sign of a blocked root. It may arise as generalized anxiety, phobias, or a constant undercurrent of unease. This fear is not always rational — it often stems from unresolved trauma, early childhood experiences, or ancestral imprints of scarcity and danger. People with blocked root energy may feel "on edge," as though the ground beneath them could collapse at any moment.

## Insecurity

When Muladhara energy is deficient, there is often a deep sense of insecurity. This can manifest as difficulty trusting others, mistrusting life itself, or doubting one's own ability to meet basic needs. Relationships, jobs, and living situations may feel unstable, reinforcing the belief that safety is fleeting or unavailable.

## Instability

Blocked root energy often shows up as life instability. This may look like frequent moves, inconsistent income, lack of routine, or difficulty holding steady commitments. The person may appear restless, never able to "put down roots." On a deeper level, this reflects the energetic instability of Muladhara itself.

## Disconnection

One of the most telling signs of a deficient Root Chakra is disconnection from the body. The individual may feel ungrounded, "out of touch," or as if they are floating outside themselves. Physical needs like eating, resting, or exercising may be ignored. Spiritually, there may be an overemphasis on higher chakras — seeking transcendence without embodiment. This disconnection prevents true spiritual growth, as higher awareness cannot be sustained without a stable foundation in the body.

**How It Feels:**

- Chronic fatigue or low vitality
- Feeling unsafe even in secure environments
- Difficulty saving or managing money
- Digestive or elimination issues
- A sense of being rootless, "homeless," or cut off from belonging

Blocked or deficient root energy is a call to **rebuild trust with the earth, the body, and life itself**. Healing begins by gently restoring safety and presence, reminding the nervous system that it is possible to feel rooted and secure again.

# Excess or Overactive Root Energy

Just as the Root Chakra can become deficient or blocked, it can also swing into **excess**. When Muladhara overcompensates, survival energy becomes amplified into rigidity, control, and attachment. Instead of providing stability, an overactive Root creates heaviness and restriction — like a tree with roots so tangled in the soil that it cannot grow upward.

**Rigidity**

An overactive Root often shows up as inflexibility. Life must be predictable, routines unchanging, and plans tightly controlled. This rigidity may bring temporary security but blocks growth, creativity, and trust in the natural flow of life. Instead of feeling grounded, the person becomes locked in place, unable to adapt to change.

## Greed and Materialism

Excessive root energy can manifest as a fixation on possessions, money, and status. The desire for material security becomes insatiable, driven not by true need but by fear of loss. Greed is a shadow response to insecurity, where accumulation replaces genuine grounding. The person may hoard resources or place their sense of safety entirely in what they own.

## Over-Control

When Muladhara energy is too strong, control becomes a way to force stability. The person may attempt to manage others, dominate environments, or over-plan every detail to prevent uncertainty. This often creates tension in relationships and reinforces fear rather than relieving it. Over-control closes the flow of energy instead of allowing it to rise naturally through the chakras.

## Aggression and Anger

In some cases, an overactive Root fuels aggression. Survival instincts, when exaggerated, can trigger a "fight" response even when no true danger is present. This may show up as irritability, defensiveness, or conflict-driven behavior. The root is meant to protect, but in excess, it becomes combative.

## How It Feels:

- Heaviness, sluggishness, or feeling "weighed down"
- Overeating or excessive attachment to food and comfort
- Hoarding possessions, money, or resources "just in case"

- Clinging to routines, jobs, or relationships out of fear of change
- Chronic tension in the lower body — hips, legs, and back

Excess root energy is not true stability. It is survival energy that has become **stuck in defense mode**. Healing involves loosening the grip, releasing fear-driven attachment, and trusting that safety comes not from control but from alignment with the natural flow of life.

# The Experience of an Imbalanced Root

When the Root Chakra is out of balance, the experience is often visceral. Because Muladhara governs survival and the physical body, its imbalance is not abstract — it shows up in the way we feel, act, and move through life. These signs can be physical, emotional, mental, and spiritual, weaving together into a sense that the ground beneath us is unstable.

**Physical Experience**

The body is the first place where an imbalance is felt. Root issues often manifest in the **lower body** — the legs, feet, hips, and lower back. Chronic tension, fatigue, digestive problems, or elimination issues may point toward Muladhara imbalance. Some people describe feeling "heavy" and sluggish, while others feel weak and disconnected from their physical strength.

**Emotional Experience**

At the emotional level, imbalance at the Root often feels like **fear, insecurity, or instability**. It can show up as constant worry, difficulty trusting others, or the sense that something is always "about to go wrong." These feelings often linger even when external circumstances are relatively stable, because the imbalance comes from within.

**Mental Experience**

The mind of an imbalanced Root tends to circle around survival. Thoughts may revolve around money, safety, work, or housing. A scarcity mindset — "there's never enough" — becomes dominant, leading to overplanning, hoarding, or obsessive worry. Conversely, in a deficient state, the mind may drift into distraction and disconnection, unable to focus or commit.

**Spiritual Experience**

On the spiritual level, imbalance at the Root can create a sense of being **ungrounded or rootless**. Instead of feeling connected to the earth and supported by life, the person may feel like they don't belong anywhere. There may be a desire to escape into higher spiritual experiences, bypassing the physical body and earthly responsibilities. But without grounding, these pursuits lack integration.

**Overall Experience**

Living with an imbalanced Root often feels like trying to build a life on shifting sand. There is no firm base from which to rest, grow, or rise. The body may ache, the mind may worry, and the heart may long for stability. These signals are not punishments, but invitations. They are reminders to return to the foundation — to reconnect with the earth, nourish the body, and reestablish safety within.

# Chapter 5 – Causes of Disturbance

## Childhood Instability and Trauma

The Root Chakra is the first to develop in childhood. Between birth and approximately seven years old, a child's sense of safety, belonging, and trust in the world is formed. If the environment is nurturing and predictable, Muladhara grows strong, creating a solid foundation for later development. But if instability, neglect, or trauma occurs, the Root Chakra may become weakened, setting patterns that persist into adulthood.

### The Role of Early Safety

Children rely entirely on their caregivers to meet their most basic needs — food, shelter, comfort, and protection. When these needs are met consistently, the child learns: *I am safe, I am cared for, I belong.* This becomes the inner foundation of the Root Chakra. But when needs are ignored, delayed, or met inconsistently, the child develops insecurity: *Am I safe? Can I trust? Do I belong?*

### Instability in the Home

Frequent moves, financial hardship, conflict, or loss of a parent can all create instability for a child. Without a stable home environment, the child's Muladhara energy may never fully root, leaving them feeling ungrounded throughout life. This can show up later as difficulty settling down, committing, or feeling at home anywhere.

**Trauma and Fear**

Experiences of trauma — such as abuse, neglect, violence, or abandonment — strike directly at the Root Chakra. Trauma sends the nervous system into survival mode, where fear, hypervigilance, or numbness become the norm. For children, who have little control over their circumstances, this survival wiring becomes deeply imprinted in the Root Chakra, shaping their sense of safety as adults.

**Effects into Adulthood**

Adults who experienced instability or trauma in childhood may notice:

- Chronic fear or anxiety without a clear cause
- Difficulty trusting others or feeling safe in relationships
- Struggles with financial stability or creating a secure home
- Feeling rootless, disconnected from family or belonging
- A tendency to live in "survival mode" even in safe circumstances

The wounded child within still seeks stability, security, and belonging. Root Chakra healing often requires reconnecting with that inner child, offering the safety and stability that was missing in the past. Through practices of grounding, self-compassion, and therapeutic support, the adult can begin to reestablish the foundation that was fractured in youth.

# Poverty, Scarcity, and Survival Stress

The Root Chakra is directly tied to how we experience **safety and security in daily life**. For many, poverty, scarcity, or prolonged survival stress can disrupt Muladhara energy, leaving deep imprints of fear and instability. Even if the material situation later improves, the energetic wound often lingers.

**Poverty and Material Insecurity**

When basic needs such as food, shelter, and clothing are uncertain, the Root Chakra is the first to feel the impact. Poverty sends the nervous system into constant survival mode: *Will I have enough to eat? Will I have a safe place to sleep? Will I be okay tomorrow?* These questions live at the heart of Muladhara, and when unanswered, they weaken the foundation of safety.

**The Scarcity Mindset**

Scarcity is not only material — it is also psychological. Even those with resources may carry the imprint of scarcity if they grew up with instability, financial fear, or family patterns of "never enough." This scarcity mindset manifests as chronic worry about money, overwork, hoarding, or difficulty trusting abundance. Instead of feeling rooted in security, life becomes an endless quest for more, fueled by fear rather than trust.

**Survival Stress**

Extended periods of survival stress — such as war, displacement, natural disasters, or economic collapse — deeply disturb the Root Chakra. These experiences reinforce fear of instability not just on a personal level, but also collectively. Communities and generations touched by such events often pass on survival anxiety to their descendants, embedding scarcity in the energetic field of entire families or cultures.

**Long-Term Effects**

Living under poverty, scarcity, or survival stress can lead to:

- Anxiety about finances, even in times of stability
- Difficulty resting or feeling safe, as the nervous system stays on alert
- Overattachment to money or possessions as substitutes for security
- Avoidance of risk or change, even when opportunities arise
- A sense of mistrust in life's ability to provide

The energy of Muladhara thrives on **trust and sufficiency**. Healing requires gently shifting from a state of "there is never enough" to "I have what I need, and life will provide." This does not dismiss the reality of hardship, but it acknowledges that grounding and security are inner states as well as outer circumstances.

# Ancestral Patterns of Fear, Migration, or Displacement

The Root Chakra is not only shaped by our personal experiences but also by the experiences of those who came before us. Survival imprints — fear, displacement, migration, or loss of homeland — can be passed down through generations, embedding themselves in the energetic foundation of families and cultures.

**Inherited Fear**

Fear is one of the strongest Root Chakra imprints. If parents or grandparents lived through wars, famines, or persecution, their nervous systems adapted to survive constant danger. Even without consciously telling the stories, they may pass down subtle cues of fear, vigilance, or mistrust. Children growing up in these families often absorb the message: *the world is not safe.*

This becomes part of their own Muladhara blueprint, even if their personal lives are stable.

## Migration and Loss of Homeland

When families are forced to migrate — whether through colonization, political upheaval, or economic hardship — a fracture occurs at the Root. Home, tribe, and land are deeply tied to Muladhara, and losing them creates feelings of rootlessness and disconnection. Descendants of displaced peoples often feel torn between cultures or struggle with a sense of "not belonging anywhere," a direct reflection of ancestral Muladhara wounds.

## Displacement and Exile

Communities who experienced exile, slavery, or systemic displacement carry collective trauma in the Root Chakra. This trauma can show up generations later as difficulty creating stability, mistrust of authority, or survival anxiety that seems "inherited." Epigenetic research now confirms what spiritual traditions have long known — trauma can leave imprints not only on memory but also on the body itself, carried forward biologically and energetically.

## How These Patterns Show Up Today

- Chronic financial worry, even when secure
- Difficulty settling in one place or constantly moving homes
- Struggles with identity and belonging across cultures
- A deep longing for "home" that is hard to define
- Feeling rootless or disconnected from ancestry and tradition

**Healing the Ancestral Root**

Healing Muladhara often involves acknowledging and honoring these ancestral stories. Rituals of remembrance, connecting with cultural traditions, and grounding practices tied to the earth can restore stability. By tending to the Root, we not only heal ourselves but also release patterns carried through generations. This allows future generations to inherit trust and rootedness instead of fear.

# Environmental and Energetic Toxins: Violence, Stress, Societal Instability

The Root Chakra is deeply sensitive to the **environment we live in**. Because Muladhara governs safety and survival, any atmosphere of violence, instability, or chronic stress registers as a threat to the foundation of being. Even if we are not in immediate danger, the collective field around us shapes how secure or insecure we feel.

**Violence and Trauma in the Environment**

Exposure to violence — whether in the home, community, or through global events — shocks the Root Chakra. The body contracts, the nervous system becomes hypervigilant, and the aura tightens. For those who experience violence directly, the imprint can be severe, leaving the Root locked in defense mode. Even witnessing violence from a distance (through media or social channels) can trigger Muladhara, especially over time.

**Chronic Stress**

Modern life often keeps the Root Chakra in a state of low-grade alarm. Fast-paced schedules, economic pressures, urban noise, and digital overstimulation send constant signals to the body that safety is under threat. While occasional stress is natural, chronic stress floods the adrenal glands, keeps the nervous system on high alert, and weakens Muladhara's stability. Instead of a foundation, the root becomes a pressure point.

## Societal Instability

When society itself feels unstable — through political upheaval, war, climate crisis, pandemics, or rapid cultural change — the Root Chakra registers collective fear. Even if personal life feels stable, the shared field of instability creates unease. This can manifest as anxiety, mistrust of systems, or difficulty envisioning a secure future. The root thrives on continuity and predictability, and when these are absent, grounding weakens.

## Energetic Toxins

Beyond the physical environment, Muladhara is also affected by energetic toxins: constant exposure to fear-based media, unhealthy group dynamics, or negative energetic fields. These influences may not threaten survival directly, but they erode inner stability by keeping fear and scarcity activated.

## The Result

Environmental and energetic toxins create a sense that life is dangerous, unpredictable, or overwhelming. Physically, this may show up as tension in the legs and lower back, digestive disturbances, or adrenal fatigue. Emotionally, it feels like restlessness, mistrust, and fear of collapse. Spiritually, it creates a disconnection from the earth and a longing for escape rather than embodiment.

Healing requires conscious choices to **detoxify the root environment** — reducing exposure to violence and fear-based messages, building supportive community, reconnecting with nature, and cultivating daily grounding rituals that remind the body: *I am safe. I am rooted. Life supports me.*

# Chapter 6 – Signs of Balance

## Emotional Stability: Safety, Trust, and Security

When the Root Chakra is balanced, life feels steady and supported. Instead of being ruled by fear, survival anxiety, or scarcity, the emotional body rests in a state of calm trust. Muladhara in harmony creates the foundation upon which the rest of the chakra system can flourish — safety in the root allows love in the heart, expression in the throat, and vision in the brow to emerge naturally.

**Safety**

Safety is the first and most important gift of a balanced root. It is not simply the absence of danger, but the inner knowing that *I am protected, I am supported, I am secure in this moment.* Even when challenges arise, the nervous system does not collapse into fear. Instead, you can respond with grounded awareness. Safety in the root feels like living in your body fully, without tension or withdrawal.

**Trust**

Trust is another sign of root balance. It is the capacity to trust yourself, your body, other people, and life itself. This trust is not blind or naïve — it is grounded in the lived experience that you can endure, adapt, and find stability. With trust in the root, relationships deepen because you are not ruled by fear of abandonment or betrayal. The world no longer feels hostile but becomes a place where belonging is possible.

## Security

Security flows naturally when Muladhara is strong. This does not mean having endless resources, but rather the confidence that your needs can and will be met. A secure Root Chakra manifests as healthy relationships with money, work, and home. Instead of obsessing over "not enough," you relax into the rhythm of sufficiency: *I have what I need, and life will continue to provide.*

## The Feeling of Emotional Stability

Together, safety, trust, and security create an emotional environment of stability. This is the opposite of survival mode. Instead of scanning for threats, the balanced Root rests, allowing energy to rise toward creativity, love, and purpose. You feel calm, centered, and anchored in the present. In this state, life no longer feels like a battle for survival, but an opportunity to grow and thrive.

# Physical Vitality: Bones, Legs, Feet, and Adrenals

The Root Chakra is the energetic foundation of the body, and when it is balanced, this strength is reflected in the physical self. Muladhara governs the **bones, legs, feet, and adrenal glands**, which together provide both structure and stamina. A healthy root creates vitality, resilience, and the ability to move through life with steadiness and power.

## Bones: The Inner Framework

Bones are the literal foundation of the body, just as Muladhara is the foundation of the chakra system. When the root is balanced, bones feel strong and supportive. This strength extends beyond the physical skeleton — it gives you the confidence to stand tall, to "have a backbone," and to move through life with integrity and resilience.

## Legs: Moving Forward with Stability

The legs carry us forward and connect us directly to the earth. Balanced root energy shows up as stability in the legs — not only the ability to stand firm but also to step forward with trust. Strong, grounded legs mirror the qualities of Muladhara: endurance, persistence, and the ability to remain steady even when life is uncertain.

## Feet: Our Sacred Connection to Earth

The feet are the body's direct contact with the earth, and they embody the grounding nature of the root. When Muladhara is balanced, your feet feel connected and alive, as though drawing nourishment from the ground beneath you. Walking barefoot on natural earth can amplify this connection, reinforcing both physical vitality and spiritual grounding.

## Adrenals: The Guardians of Survival

The adrenal glands, located above the kidneys, regulate the body's response to stress. In a balanced Root Chakra, the adrenals function smoothly — able to activate in moments of real danger but also able to rest when the threat has passed. This creates resilience rather than burnout. When the root is balanced, you feel steady, energized, and alert without being trapped in constant fight-or-flight.

**The Feeling of Physical Vitality**

With a balanced Muladhara, vitality flows through the body. There is a sense of strength in the bones, power in the legs, connection in the feet, and resilience in the adrenals. The physical self feels like a trustworthy home — capable of supporting, protecting, and carrying you through life.

# The Body as a Mirror of the Root

The Root Chakra is the gateway between spirit and body. When balanced, it reflects harmony in the physical self — not only in strength and stamina but in the way we inhabit our body as a whole. The body becomes a mirror of the Root, showing us whether we are grounded, safe, and secure in our lives.

**Posture and Presence**

A balanced root reveals itself in posture. The spine feels aligned, the legs steady, the feet planted with ease. You stand and move with natural confidence, as though the earth itself is supporting you. By contrast, slouching, collapsing, or shuffling movements may indicate root imbalance — the body unconsciously mirroring instability.

**Vitality and Endurance**

The body of a grounded person exudes vitality. Energy flows evenly, creating stamina and the ability to sustain effort without strain. Just as a tree draws nourishment through its roots, a balanced Muladhara allows the body to draw steady energy from the earth. This creates resilience, health, and the ability to bounce back after a challenge.

## Comfort in the Body

When the Root Chakra is strong, you feel at home in your own body. There is ease in movement, comfort in stillness, and trust in your physical presence. Instead of trying to escape the body or ignore its needs, you treat it as a sacred dwelling. This comfort translates into self-confidence and stability in daily life.

## Grounded Awareness

The body mirrors the Root in how present you feel. A grounded person is attentive to their senses — they notice the texture of the ground beneath their feet, the rhythm of their breath, the support of the chair beneath them. This awareness creates a calm, embodied presence that radiates to others.

## Health as Reflection

Imbalances in the Root often show up in the body first — in the lower back, legs, feet, or adrenal fatigue. Conversely, when Muladhara is balanced, health in these areas tends to stabilize. The body reflects security, resilience, and balance, showing that the energetic foundation is strong.

## The Lesson of the Body

The body is always speaking, and its language often reflects the state of the Root Chakra. By listening to posture, vitality, comfort, awareness, and health, we can see clearly whether we are grounded or ungrounded. The body is not separate from spirit — it is the living mirror of Muladhara's energy.

# Spiritual Qualities: Groundedness, Belonging, and Connection to Earth

When the Root Chakra is balanced, spirituality is not an escape from life — it is an **embodied presence** within it. Muladhara teaches that enlightenment does not come only from rising upward, but from rooting deeply into the earth. This grounded spirituality provides a sense of belonging and a sacred connection to the living world.

## Groundedness

Groundedness is the felt sense that you are fully present in this moment, inhabiting both body and spirit with ease. It is the ability to stand steady even when life shifts, to remain calm in uncertainty, and to feel the earth supporting you with every step. A grounded person radiates stability — their presence alone can calm others because they are rooted in trust.

## Belonging

A balanced Root Chakra awakens the spiritual truth of belonging. You no longer feel like an outsider to life but as part of the greater whole — family, community, humanity, and nature itself. Belonging at Muladhara dissolves the illusion of isolation. You recognize that survival is not a solitary act but a shared experience, and that you are held by the web of life.

## Connection to Earth

The deepest spiritual quality of Muladhara is connection to the earth. You feel yourself not as separate from nature but as part of it. Walking barefoot, tending soil, sitting beneath trees, or simply breathing fresh air becomes a form of prayer. The earth is not just your environment — it is your **foundation, partner, and teacher.**

## The Spiritual Gift of the Root

Spirituality at the root is simple yet profound: to be alive is sacred. To eat, to walk, to breathe, to rest — these are not mundane acts but holy expressions of life itself. Muladhara reminds us that before we seek transcendence, we must honor embodiment. The gift of the Root Chakra is the realization that heaven is not only above but also beneath our feet.

# The Experience of a Balanced Root

Living with a balanced Root Chakra is like standing on solid ground after years of uncertainty. There is an unmistakable sense of **ease, trust, and vitality** that permeates every aspect of life. You no longer feel as though you must fight for survival — instead, you experience life as supportive, abundant, and safe.

### Physical Experience

The body feels strong, stable, and energized. The legs and feet carry you with confidence, the bones feel resilient, and the nervous system rests in equilibrium. You feel at home in your body, aware of its signals and needs, and grateful for its strength.

### Emotional Experience

Emotionally, there is a deep sense of safety and steadiness. Fear and worry no longer dominate. Instead, trust arises naturally — in yourself, in others, and in life. You are not ruled by scarcity or insecurity but rest in the assurance that your needs will be met.

## Mental Experience

The mind of a balanced root is calm and focused. Rather than obsessing about survival, money, or safety, you can concentrate on growth, creativity, and higher purpose. Stability at Muladhara creates mental clarity and the ability to make grounded decisions without panic or distraction.

## Spiritual Experience

Spiritually, the experience is one of belonging. You feel connected to the earth, to your community, and to the larger web of life. You recognize yourself as part of creation, supported by the rhythms of nature. This connection transforms spirituality from an abstract pursuit into a lived reality — every breath, every step, every heartbeat is sacred.

## Overall Experience

With a balanced Root Chakra, life feels rooted yet expansive. You are steady in the body, calm in the mind, open in the heart, and aligned with the earth. This foundation allows the higher chakras to awaken safely, knowing they are supported from below.

A balanced root is not just the absence of fear — it is the presence of **confidence, vitality, and trust in life itself.**

# Chapter 7 – Hidden Secrets & Esoteric Wisdom

## Tantra and the Root Chakra

The ancient yogic texts describe Muladhara not only as the seat of survival but also as the **gateway to profound spiritual awakening**. Within Tantra, the Root Chakra is regarded as the home of **Kundalini Shakti**, the dormant serpent energy coiled at the base of the spine. While most people experience Muladhara primarily through survival instincts, Tantric teachings view it as the threshold where the material and spiritual worlds meet.

**Kundalini at the Root**

In Tantric philosophy, Kundalini rests in Muladhara in a state of dormancy, coiled three and a half times around the base of the spine. Awakening this energy is said to ignite the journey of consciousness up through the chakras, uniting with **Shiva** (pure consciousness) at the crown. Yet Tantra emphasizes that the journey cannot begin until the Root is stable. Without grounding, the rising of Kundalini can be destabilizing rather than liberating.

## The Sacredness of the Physical Body

Tantra does not treat the body as an obstacle to spirituality but as a sacred vessel. The Root Chakra embodies this principle. It is through the body — its bones, instincts, and connection to the earth — that we access the divine. Muladhara reminds us that spirit does not bypass matter; it *incarnates* through it. Thus, caring for the body, honoring sexuality, and embracing earthly life are seen as spiritual practices within Tantra.

## The Polarity of Shakti and Shiva

The downward-pointing triangle of the Root Chakra symbolizes the feminine principle — grounding, nourishment, and receptivity. This is Shakti, the divine creative force. In Tantra, Shakti at the root is not lesser than Shiva at the crown; both are necessary for wholeness. The path of awakening begins by honoring Shakti at Muladhara, for only through her grounding power can consciousness safely rise to meet Shiva.

## Tantric Practices for Muladhara

Traditional Tantric practices include:

- **Bija Mantra:** Chanting *LAM* to awaken the vibrational essence of the root.
- **Yantra Meditation:** Visualizing the square and downward triangle of Muladhara to stabilize the mind.
- **Breathwork:** Rooted breathing into the base of the spine, drawing energy downward before allowing it to rise.
- **Sacred Rituals:** Honoring the earth, sexuality, and the body as sacred expressions of Shakti.

## The Secret Wisdom

The hidden Tantric wisdom of the Root is this: **the journey upward begins by going down.** Awakening is not about escaping the body but descending into it fully, rooting deeply into earth and matter until the divine reveals itself through physical existence. The Root Chakra is not the lowest point of spirituality — it is the threshold to liberation.

# Kundalini: Dormant Serpent Energy and Its Awakening

At the very base of the Root Chakra lies one of the most profound teachings of yogic and Tantric tradition: **Kundalini Shakti**. This energy is often depicted as a **serpent coiled three and a half times**, resting in dormancy within Muladhara. Though unseen, it is the latent force of consciousness — the seed of enlightenment sleeping at the root of the spine.

### The Dormant Serpent

The image of the serpent reflects primal power — instinctual, fertile, and mysterious. Just as a snake coils and waits, Kundalini is said to lie still until awakened by practice, devotion, or life's initiations. In this dormant state, the energy of Kundalini is both protective and potential-filled. It guards the gateway of Muladhara, ensuring that the ascent of consciousness does not occur prematurely.

### The Awakening

When conditions are right — when the Root Chakra is stable, the nadis (energy channels) are open, and the practitioner is grounded — Kundalini begins to uncoil. This awakening is often described as a surge of energy rising up through the central channel (*sushumna nadi*), piercing each chakra in turn, and ultimately uniting with **Shiva** at the crown. The experience can bring profound states of bliss, expanded consciousness, and spiritual realization.

**Signs of Rising Energy**

Accounts of Kundalini awakening often include sensations such as:

- Heat or tingling at the base of the spine
- Energy moving upward through the back or central channel
- Spontaneous body movements or postures (known as *kriyas*)
- Vivid dreams or heightened intuition
- A deep sense of unity with the earth, body, and cosmos

These signs vary widely from person to person, as Kundalini awakens in ways tailored to each individual's path.

**The Importance of Grounding**

While Kundalini is a source of liberation, ancient texts caution that awakening it prematurely or without grounding can destabilize the body and mind. Unbalanced ascents may lead to anxiety, disorientation, or physical symptoms. This is why Tantric and yogic masters emphasize beginning with Muladhara. Only when the root is steady can the serpent rise safely.

**The Secret Wisdom of Kundalini**

The greatest mystery of Kundalini is that it does not awaken by force — it awakens by **readiness**. Devotion, self-awareness, and consistent practice cultivate the conditions for the serpent to stir. The awakening is not a conquest but a surrender, an invitation for Shakti to rise and reveal the divine nature within.

Muladhara is the resting place of this sacred power, reminding us that our survival instincts and spiritual awakening are not separate. They are two expressions of the same root energy — one for living, the other for transcending.

# Karmic Lessons of Survival Across Lifetimes

The Root Chakra not only carries the imprint of our current life but also holds echoes of **karmic lessons from previous incarnations**. Because Muladhara governs survival, belonging, and safety, unresolved patterns in these areas often reappear across lifetimes, calling for healing and integration.

### The Cycle of Survival

In many spiritual traditions, survival challenges are viewed as karmic tests. A soul that experienced poverty, war, or displacement in one lifetime may carry the energetic imprint into the next. These memories often surface as unexplained fears, scarcity mindsets, or persistent feelings of rootlessness. They are not punishments but opportunities — invitations to meet survival differently, with greater trust and awareness.

### Patterns of Fear and Instability

Fear of loss, abandonment, or not having enough may feel stronger than present circumstances warrant. This can be a sign of karmic residue. For example:

- A person may feel terrified of homelessness even while financially secure.

- Another may struggle to settle in one place, echoing past lives of migration or exile.
- Others may carry deep mistrust of authority, reflecting ancestral or karmic memories of persecution.

These patterns reveal the karmic lessons of Muladhara: to face fear not as an enemy, but as a teacher that guides us toward deeper grounding and self-trust.

## Belonging Across Lifetimes

Belonging is another recurring karmic theme. Souls who were excluded from community, tribe, or family in past lives may reincarnate with strong desires to find connection — or with deep fears of rejection. Healing the Root means remembering that belonging is not only external but also internal: we belong to ourselves, to the earth, and to the greater soul journey we share with others.

## Breaking the Karmic Cycle

The karmic lessons of the Root Chakra always point toward **integration**. Each lifetime offers a chance to release fear, rebuild stability, and embody trust in the earth's support. Through grounding practices, ancestral healing, and conscious awareness, we begin to dissolve karmic imprints. This frees not only ourselves but also our lineage and future generations from repeating survival-based struggles.

## The Hidden Gift

The hidden gift of these karmic lessons is that they reveal survival as sacred. Each time a soul works through fear, scarcity, or instability, it anchors deeper wisdom into the Root Chakra. Lifetime after lifetime, the soul learns that survival is not just about enduring life but about rooting spirit in matter —

creating a foundation strong enough to carry consciousness toward liberation.

# Secret Uses of the Root: Shamanic Journeys, Earth Bonding, and Primal Power

Beyond its visible role in survival and grounding, the Root Chakra carries hidden potentials that spiritual traditions across the world have quietly honored. These **secret uses** reveal Muladhara not just as the foundation of human life, but as a gateway into deeper wisdom, primal strength, and mystical connection with the earth itself.

### Shamanic Journeys

In shamanic traditions, the base of the spine is often seen as the **portal to the Lower World** — a realm of ancestral spirits, animal guides, and earth wisdom. Practitioners enter this world by journeying down through an imagined tunnel, cave, or tree roots. This descent mirrors the Root Chakra's function: to connect us with hidden sources of power below the surface. Through Muladhara, shamans access ancestral knowledge, recover soul fragments, and gain survival wisdom for both themselves and their communities. The Root thus becomes a sacred doorway, not only for personal grounding but also for spiritual exploration and healing.

### Earth Bonding

The Root Chakra is our energetic tether to the earth. Ancient practices emphasized direct contact — walking barefoot on soil, sitting against trees, burying hands in the ground — as a way to charge the body with the earth's electromagnetic energy. Modern science now confirms that "earthing" or "grounding" helps regulate the nervous system, reduce stress, and restore vitality.

Spiritually, earth bonding through Muladhara dissolves the illusion of separation. You no longer feel like a visitor on the planet but as part of her body. This bond creates a sense of reverence for the natural world and deepens your role as caretaker of the earth.

## Primal Power

The Root Chakra holds **primal life force energy** — the raw vitality that fuels instinct, endurance, and resilience. While higher chakras are associated with refinement, Muladhara reminds us that spirituality begins with raw power. This primal force can be channeled into strength, sexual vitality, creativity, and determination. In Tantric traditions, this is the very energy that fuels Kundalini's ascent.

When accessed consciously, primal power is not chaotic or destructive but deeply life-affirming. It provides the stamina to survive challenges, the vitality to thrive, and the courage to embrace life fully.

## The Hidden Wisdom

The secret uses of the Root Chakra show us that grounding is not a limitation — it is empowerment. Shamanic descent, earth bonding, and primal vitality all point toward the same truth: **the deeper you root, the higher you can rise.** By honoring Muladhara as both foundation and gateway, you unlock not only survival but the ancient power hidden within the earth and your own body.

# Western Mysticism: Root as the Foundation of the Temple

In the Western esoteric traditions, the imagery of the **foundation** appears again and again — echoing the same truths carried in Muladhara. Though the language differs, the essence remains: without a strong base, no structure, whether physical or spiritual, can endure.

**The Foundation Stone**

In Jewish mysticism, the Kabbalistic *sefirah* known as **Malkuth** ("Kingdom") represents the material world — the ground of manifestation and the starting point of spiritual ascent. Malkuth is often described as the foundation stone of the temple, paralleling the Root Chakra as the base that supports higher states of consciousness. Just as Muladhara connects us to earth, Malkuth grounds divine energy in form.

**The Temple as the Body**

Christian mysticism often describes the body as a **temple of the Holy Spirit**, built upon a foundation of faith. Early texts liken Christ to the cornerstone upon which the entire spiritual edifice rests. This mirrors the role of Muladhara: the cornerstone of the human energy temple. Without it, the "temple" of body, mind, and spirit cannot stand firm.

**Alchemy and the Element of Earth**

In alchemy, the **element of earth** is linked with salt — the principle of solidity, preservation, and form. Alchemical transformation begins with grounding in earth before progressing to the higher elements of fire, water, and air. The alchemical maxim *Visita Interiora Terrae* ("Visit the interior of the earth") reminds us that true transformation begins by going downward — into earth, body, and matter — just as Muladhara is the first step on the journey upward through the chakras.

## Masonic Symbolism

In Freemasonry, the Temple of Solomon represents the spiritual structure each initiate must build within themselves. The very first lessons emphasize **laying a firm foundation** before constructing the higher temple. The square — also the geometric symbol within the Root Chakra lotus — is a sacred tool of Masons, representing stability, grounding, and alignment.

## The Shared Wisdom

Across Western mysticism, the teaching is consistent: the foundation is not optional, it is essential. Just as Muladhara roots the chakra system, the cornerstone or foundation stone roots the temple of spirit. The lesson is clear: spiritual ascent requires a grounded base, and matter itself is holy when recognized as the dwelling place of the divine.

# Chapter 8 – Balancing & Healing Practices

## Reiki Positions and Energy Protocols for the Root

Because the Root Chakra governs safety, survival, and grounding, Reiki practitioners often begin or end their sessions by focusing here. The Root anchors the flow of life force energy (*ki* or *prana*), and balancing it ensures that higher chakras can open without destabilizing the client.

**Hand Positions for the Root Chakra**

Reiki hand placements for Muladhara are generally located at or near the **base of the spine, hips, and feet**. Practitioners may choose positions depending on comfort and client preference:

- **Base of the Spine:** Hands gently placed near the coccyx (with client consent, usually with a respectful hover rather than direct contact).
- **Hips and Pelvis:** Placing hands on each hip helps balance the energy channels that flow downward into the legs.
- **Legs and Knees:** Hands placed along the thighs or knees encourage grounding and stability.
- **Feet:** Placing hands over the tops or soles of the feet helps "seal" the energy session, anchoring healing into the earth.

## Energy Protocols

1. **Grounding the Session:** Practitioners often begin with the Root, drawing Reiki energy downward to anchor the client into the treatment space. This helps restless or anxious clients feel calm and secure.
2. **Balancing Flow:** Reiki is directed to the lower spine and hips, ensuring that energy is distributed evenly into both legs. A balanced flow between the left (feminine/receptive) and right (masculine/active) sides creates stability in daily life.
3. **Clearing Fear:** Practitioners may sense heaviness or stagnant energy around the Root. By holding the base position longer and channeling Reiki until warmth or flow returns, fear-based blockages can be released.
4. **Sealing with the Feet:** Ending the session at the feet is a common practice. This grounds the client, preventing dizziness or disorientation, and reconnects them to the earth's stabilizing energy.

## Symbolic Support

Advanced Reiki practitioners may also use Reiki symbols:

- **Cho Ku Rei** (Power Symbol) to strengthen and stabilize the Root.
- **Sei He Ki** (Harmony Symbol) if fear or emotional trauma is present.
- **Dai Ko Myo** (Master Symbol) to bring deeper spiritual grounding when working with karmic or ancestral root imbalances.

## The Practitioner's Role

Working with Muladhara in Reiki requires sensitivity. Because the Root is tied to survival and vulnerability, clients may unconsciously store trauma here. The practitioner's calm presence, respect for boundaries, and intentional grounding help create the safety needed for healing to occur.

**Healing Reminder:** Reiki at the Root is not just about releasing blocks — it is about teaching the body and soul to remember: *You are safe. You belong. You are supported by the earth beneath you.*

# Bridging the Root Chakra to the Heart Chakra

The chakras are not separate systems; they are an interconnected flow of energy. The journey from Muladhara (Root) to Anahata (Heart) is especially significant, for it represents the path from **survival to love, from fear to trust, from grounding to expansion.**

**The Path from Root to Heart**

- **Root (Muladhara):** Safety, security, survival, and connection to the earth.
- **Sacral (Svadhisthana):** Pleasure, creativity, and emotional flow.
- **Solar Plexus (Manipura):** Confidence, willpower, and personal identity.
- **Heart (Anahata):** Love, compassion, and unity.

Energy must rise through the Root, Sacral, and Solar Plexus before it can fully open in the Heart. Without grounding at the Root, love at the Heart can feel unstable, unanchored, or conditional. Conversely, when the Root is strong, the Heart can open with trust, creating relationships and compassion that rest on a solid foundation.

## Why the Bridge Matters

- A person with a strong **Root but a closed Heart** may feel safe but struggle to connect emotionally, clinging to survival without love.
- A person with an open **Heart but a weak Root** may give endlessly but feel ungrounded, insecure, or easily destabilized.
- The bridge between them ensures that love is not naïve and survival is not cold — they harmonize into a life of stability and compassion.

## Practices for Root–Heart Integration

1. **Grounded Breath into the Heart**
   - Sit comfortably and place one hand on your lower belly (Root) and the other over your chest (Heart).
   - Inhale into the belly first, then let the breath rise into the chest.
   - Exhale slowly, imagining the breath flowing back down into the Root.
   - Repeat, visualizing energy traveling up and down, weaving Root and Heart together.
2. **Walking Meditation with Gratitude**
   - As you walk, focus first on your feet grounding into the earth.
   - With each step, silently say: *I am safe. I belong.*
   - Then bring attention to your chest and say: *I am loved. I connect.*
   - This practice links the act of survival (walking, moving forward) with the act of loving presence.
3. **Crystal Grid for Root–Heart Balance**
   - Place grounding stones like hematite or black tourmaline near your feet.
   - Place heart-opening stones like rose quartz or green aventurine over your chest.

   o   Meditate with both, allowing the contrast of
       earth and love to harmonize within you.
4. **Affirmations for the Bridge**
   o   *My body is safe, my heart is open.*
   o   *I root into the earth, I rise into love.*
   o   *Survival and compassion coexist within me.*

**The Hidden Wisdom of the Bridge**

The bridge from Root to Heart teaches that love is not fragile —
it is rooted in strength. Survival energy becomes sacred when it
flows upward into compassion, and love becomes enduring
when it rests on the foundation of safety. Together, Root and
Heart embody the wholeness of being human: grounded in
earth, open in spirit.

# Bridging Root to Heart Across Cultures

Across cultures, the journey from survival to love has always
been recognized as essential to human wholeness. The Root
Chakra provides safety and survival, while the Heart awakens
compassion and connection. Together, they form the
**foundation of belonging** — to the earth, to family, to
community, and to spirit.

- **Yogic Tradition**: The chakras are seen as a ladder of
  consciousness. Root (Muladhara) anchors survival, and
  only when this foundation is secure can energy rise to
  Anahata, where love and compassion blossom. Yogis
  describe this as the transformation of *bhukti* (need) into
  *bhakti* (devotion).
- **Shamanic Practices**: Many shamanic journeys begin
  with a descent into the underworld (Root), retrieving
  survival wisdom, before ascending into the world of
  spirit (Heart). The integration of both realms ensures
  that love and healing are grounded, not abstract.

- **Indigenous Wisdom**: Tribal traditions often emphasize belonging to land (Root) and tribe (Heart). Survival and connection are not separate — they are interdependent. To live in harmony with the earth is both to survive and to love.
- **Buddhist Teachings**: While the root of suffering is attachment, balance is found in grounding mindfulness (Root) before cultivating compassion (*karuṇā*) and loving-kindness (*mettā*) of the Heart. The body is stabilized so the heart can open.
- **Western Mysticism**: Christian mystics describe faith as a cornerstone (Root) that allows love — expressed as *agape* — to expand outward. The strong foundation of faith secures the higher virtue of divine love.

## The Common Thread

No matter the culture, the bridge from Root to Heart teaches the same truth: **love cannot flourish without safety, and survival is incomplete without compassion.** The Root and Heart are not separate energies but partners on the path to wholeness.

# Meditation & Visualization Exercises for Grounding

Meditation is one of the most direct ways to balance the Root Chakra. Because Muladhara is tied to the body and the earth, grounding meditations emphasize **anchoring, stability, and presence.** Visualization strengthens this process by engaging the mind's imagery to create a felt sense of rootedness.

## Rooted Tree Visualization

1. Sit comfortably with your feet on the ground or cross-legged on the floor.

2. Close your eyes and take several deep breaths, focusing on the base of your spine.
3. Imagine roots growing downward from your spine, hips, and feet into the earth.
    o See them reaching deeper and deeper, spreading wide, wrapping around rocks and soil.
4. As you inhale, visualize drawing energy up through these roots into your body.
5. As you exhale, imagine sending any fear, stress, or instability down into the earth to be absorbed and transformed.
6. Continue for 5–10 minutes, until you feel steady and calm.

*Affirmation to repeat silently:*
*"I am rooted, I am safe, I am supported by the earth beneath me."*

**Red Lotus Grounding Meditation**

1. Sit or lie down and bring awareness to the base of your spine.
2. Visualize a glowing red lotus flower opening at Muladhara. See its four petals unfurling in vibrant, radiant light.
3. With each breath, the lotus expands, filling your lower body with warmth and stability.
4. Imagine the petals anchoring you like four pillars — in the four directions — giving you a sense of unshakable foundation.
5. Allow the red light to spread down into your legs and feet, rooting you to the earth.

**Body-Scan Grounding Practice**

This meditation uses awareness of the body to bring the mind into the present.

1. Lie flat on your back or sit with a straight spine.
2. Bring attention to your feet. Notice sensations — warmth, tingling, contact with the ground.
3. Slowly move awareness upward through your legs, hips, and lower spine, pausing to breathe into each part.
4. With each exhale, imagine releasing tension or fear; with each inhale, imagine stability filling that area.
5. When you reach the base of the spine, rest your awareness there for several minutes, simply breathing into Muladhara.

## Sound Healing for the Root Chakra

Because chakras are vibrational energy centers, sound is one of the most direct and powerful ways to restore harmony to Muladhara. The Root Chakra resonates with **deep, grounding tones** that mirror the earth's frequency — steady, slow, and anchoring. Sound bypasses the thinking mind, communicating directly with the body and energy field, reminding us of our innate connection to stability and survival.

## The Bija Mantra: LAM

Each chakra has a *bija mantra* (seed sound), and for Muladhara, the sound is **LAM** (pronounced "lahm").

- Chanting *LAM* produces a low, resonant vibration that settles into the pelvic floor and base of the spine.
- This vibration stimulates the Root Chakra, releasing fear and drawing awareness into the body.
- A simple practice is to sit comfortably, inhale deeply, and on the exhale chant **LAM** slowly, allowing the sound to vibrate through your body. Repeat for several minutes, noticing how your lower body feels more alive and grounded.

*Affirmation to pair with chanting:*
*"With every sound, I root deeper into the safety of the earth."*

## Drumming and Rhythm

In shamanic and indigenous traditions, drumming has long been used to connect with the earth and awaken primal energy.

- Steady, repetitive beats mimic the sound of the heartbeat and the rhythm of the earth.
- Listening to or playing a drum creates entrainment — the body and mind naturally synchronize with the rhythm, inducing relaxation and grounding.
- Practicing grounding with a frame drum, djembe, or recorded drumming tracks can calm the nervous system and anchor awareness in the present.

## Low Frequencies and Vibrations

The Root Chakra resonates strongly with **low-frequency sounds** (between 20–60 Hz). These deep tones can be felt as much as heard.

- Instruments like gongs, bass singing bowls, didgeridoos, or tuning forks tuned to low frequencies can activate Muladhara.
- Simply lying near such instruments allows the vibrations to move through the body, stimulating the bones, muscles, and Root Chakra center.
- Many practitioners also use recorded low-frequency soundscapes (often called "earth tones" or "grounding tracks") for meditation or sleep.

## Why Sound Works for the Root

Sound healing reconnects us to rhythm — the rhythm of heartbeat, of earth's pulse, of life itself. By resonating with

Muladhara through *LAM*, drumming, and low frequencies, we remind the body and spirit of their innate stability. This is sound not just for listening, but for **feeling** — a reminder that we are safe, supported, and rooted.

# Crystals for the Root Chakra

Crystals are natural allies for Root Chakra healing because they carry the **dense, grounding vibration of the earth**. Their mineral structure resonates with stability, endurance, and protection — exactly the qualities Muladhara requires to stay balanced. Using crystals helps anchor the body, calm the mind, and strengthen the energetic foundation.

### Hematite

- **Qualities:** Grounding, protection, stability.
- Hematite is known for its reflective, metallic surface and its ability to absorb and neutralize negative energy. It acts like a shield, strengthening the aura and anchoring you firmly into the earth.
- **Use:** Place hematite at your feet during meditation, carry it in your pocket when feeling scattered, or hold it while practicing grounding breaths.

### Red Jasper

- **Qualities:** Strength, endurance, vitality.
- Called the "stone of endurance," red jasper supports the Root Chakra by stimulating physical energy and determination. It restores stability in times of stress and builds confidence to move forward.
- **Use:** Place red jasper on the lower abdomen or base of the spine, wear it as jewelry for ongoing vitality, or use it in crystal grids for strength and security.

## Garnet

- **Qualities:** Passion, life force, courage.
- Garnet awakens the primal energy of the Root, stimulating both physical vitality and emotional courage. It is especially powerful for rekindling motivation when survival fears or fatigue drain energy.
- **Use:** Meditate with garnet near the perineum or pelvic area, carry it during times of transition, or place it under your pillow for support during change.

## Smoky Quartz

- **Qualities:** Transmutation, grounding, release of fear.
- Smoky quartz is a gentle but powerful crystal that absorbs negativity and transforms it into stability. It anchors scattered energy and helps dissolve survival anxiety.
- **Use:** Hold smoky quartz in both hands while visualizing fear draining into the stone. Place it near doorways or under the bed for protection and grounding.

## How to Work with Root Crystals

- **Placement:** Lay crystals at the feet, knees, or base of the spine during meditation or energy sessions.
- **Carrying:** Keep small tumbled stones in a pocket or bag for ongoing grounding.
- **Grids:** Combine multiple root stones in a square or circular pattern to amplify grounding energy.
- **Affirmation:** As you work with a crystal, repeat: *"I root into the earth and draw stability, strength, and safety into my body."*

Crystals do not replace grounding practices but **enhance them**, serving as physical reminders of the earth's support. Each stone is like a fragment of the Root itself — ancient, steady, and unshakable.

# Essential Oils for the Root Chakra

The Root Chakra responds deeply to **earthy, woody, and resinous scents**. These aromas connect us to the grounding presence of the natural world, calming the nervous system and anchoring awareness into the body. Essential oils can be used in meditation, massage, baths, or diffusers to awaken Muladhara and restore stability.

### Cedarwood

- **Qualities:** Stability, courage, and ancestral connection.
- Cedarwood has been used in sacred rituals for centuries to purify and protect. Its warm, woody scent fosters inner strength and steadiness, helping to dissolve feelings of fear or disconnection.
- **Use:** Diffuse cedarwood during meditation or apply (diluted) to the soles of the feet to anchor energy.

### Vetiver

- **Qualities:** Deep grounding, calming, restorative.
- Known as the "oil of tranquility," vetiver comes from the roots of a grass, making it especially resonant with Muladhara. Its earthy aroma slows racing thoughts and draws energy downward into the body.
- **Use:** Add a drop to carrier oil and massage into the lower spine, or inhale directly from the bottle when feeling anxious or unsteady.

## Patchouli

- **Qualities:** Earth connection, sensual grounding, presence.
- Patchouli's rich, musky scent connects body and mind, reminding us to stay present. It balances excess Root energy (over-control, rigidity) by softening and grounding with sensual awareness.
- **Use:** Blend with vetiver or sandalwood in a diffuser for meditation, or wear as a grounding perfume when feeling scattered.

## Sandalwood

- **Qualities:** Sacred grounding, spiritual alignment, calm strength.
- Sandalwood has long been used in temples and rituals for its ability to ground while also lifting consciousness. It bridges the Root and higher chakras, supporting both stability and devotion.
- **Use:** Apply diluted sandalwood oil to the heart and base of the spine before meditation, or burn sandalwood incense to create a grounded, sacred atmosphere.

## How to Use Root Chakra Oils

- **Diffusion:** Add a few drops to a diffuser to create a grounding environment.
- **Massage:** Mix with a carrier oil and apply to the lower back, hips, or feet.
- **Bath Ritual:** Add 3–5 drops to bath salts for a calming soak.
- **Meditation:** Place a drop on the palms, rub together, and inhale deeply before grounding practices.

*Affirmation to pair with aromatherapy:*
*"With each breath, I ground deeper into the earth and feel safe,*
*steady, and supported."*

Essential oils help bridge the physical body with the energetic body, reminding us through scent that **safety and belonging are always accessible.**

# Somatic Practices: Stomping, Walking Barefoot, Bodywork

Because the Root Chakra governs the body's connection to the earth, physical practices are among the most effective ways to restore its balance. Somatic (body-centered) methods remind us that safety and grounding are not abstract concepts but lived, felt experiences in muscles, bones, and breath.

## Stomping

- Stomping awakens Muladhara by sending rhythmic vibrations through the feet and legs, directly stimulating the nervous system and the base of the spine.
- This primal movement echoes ancient tribal dances that were used for grounding, celebration, and releasing fear.
- **Practice:** Stand with feet hip-width apart. Take slow, intentional stomps into the ground, exhaling sharply with each impact. Imagine excess fear, anger, or instability leaving your body and sinking into the earth. Continue for 1–2 minutes, then pause and notice the tingling aliveness in your legs and feet.

## Walking Barefoot (Earthing)

- Walking barefoot, also called "earthing," restores direct electrical connection with the earth. Modern research shows it helps regulate circadian rhythms, reduce stress, and balance inflammation.

- Spiritually, barefoot walking reminds us of our bond with nature, creating a sense of belonging.
- **Practice:** Walk slowly on grass, soil, or sand. With each step, consciously feel the earth pressing against your soles. Breathe deeply, imagining roots extending into the ground. Repeat affirmations such as: *"I belong to this earth."*

## Bodywork

- The Root Chakra is stored in the hips, legs, and lower spine — areas where tension and trauma often accumulate. Bodywork practices like massage, reflexology, shiatsu, or acupressure help release stagnant energy and restore flow.
- **Focus Areas:**
  - **Feet & Ankles:** Release fear and instability.
  - **Legs:** Encourage strength and movement forward.
  - **Hips & Lower Back:** Free survival stress and ancestral weight.
- **Practice:** During massage or self-massage, breathe into tight areas and visualize red light spreading warmth and stability. Pair with grounding oils like vetiver or patchouli for added effect.

## The Wisdom of Somatic Grounding

These practices remind us that healing the Root is not only energetic or symbolic — it is deeply **physical**. By moving, feeling, and reconnecting with the earth through the body, we embody the essence of Muladhara: *to live grounded, safe, and fully present in the here and now.*

# Yoga and Breathwork for the Root Chakra

Yoga and conscious breathing are powerful allies for balancing Muladhara because they bring awareness directly into the body's foundation. Root-focused poses and breath practices cultivate stability, calm the nervous system, and anchor energy into the lower body.

**Yoga Asanas for the Root Chakra**

Grounding postures emphasize **connection to the earth, strong foundations, and opening the hips and legs.**

- **Mountain Pose (Tadasana):**
  Standing tall with feet firmly planted, this pose builds awareness of stability and alignment. Imagine roots growing from your feet deep into the ground.
- **Warrior II (Virabhadrasana II):**
  Strengthens the legs and hips while creating a wide, rooted stance. Focus on drawing power from the earth into your body.
- **Garland Pose (Malasana Squat):**
  Opens the hips and brings the body close to the earth. This posture releases tension in the pelvis and encourages grounding energy.
- **Bridge Pose (Setu Bandhasana):**
  Strengthens the lower back, glutes, and legs while opening the pelvic floor — directly stimulating the Root Chakra.
- **Child's Pose (Balasana):**
  A deeply grounding, restful posture that brings the torso to the earth, calming fear and anxiety.

*Tip:* Hold each Root-centered asana for several deep breaths, visualizing a red glow at the base of the spine.

## Breathwork for Muladhara

Breathing deeply into the lower belly and pelvis awakens Root energy and signals safety to the body.

- **Dirgha Pranayama (Three-Part Breath):**
  Begin with slow, full breaths, first expanding the belly, then the ribs, then the chest. This sequence roots awareness into the lower body before lifting it upward.
- **Root Lock Breath (Mula Bandha):**
  Engage the pelvic floor muscles gently as you inhale, hold, then release on the exhale. This practice strengthens awareness of Muladhara and stimulates energy flow at the base of the spine.
- **4-8 Grounding Breath:**
  Inhale for a count of 4, exhale slowly for a count of 8. The extended exhale activates the parasympathetic nervous system, calming fear and grounding the body.

## Integration Practice

Combine yoga and breathwork for deeper grounding:

- Begin in **Mountain Pose**, inhaling deeply into the belly.
- Transition into **Warrior II**, exhaling with strength into the legs.
- Flow into **Malasana Squat**, breathing deeply into the hips.
- End in **Child's Pose**, practicing the 4-8 Grounding Breath.

**Affirmation to pair with practice:**
*"With each breath and movement, I root deeper into stability, strength, and safety."*

# Food Therapy: Root Vegetables, Protein, Earthy Foods

Because the Root Chakra governs the body's survival instincts, food is one of the most direct ways to bring balance. Eating with awareness — choosing foods that resonate with earth energy — strengthens Muladhara by supporting both physical vitality and the sense of being nourished and safe.

## Root Vegetables

- Foods that grow underground carry the stabilizing, grounding energy of the earth.
- Examples: carrots, beets, potatoes, parsnips, turnips, onions, garlic.
- Their dense, hearty qualities anchor energy in the body, providing a sense of warmth and security.
- **Practice:** Prepare roasted root vegetables with earthy herbs (rosemary, thyme) as a grounding meal. As you eat, visualize drawing strength from the earth's nourishment.

## Protein for Strength and Stability

- Protein-rich foods build muscle, repair tissues, and support stamina — all vital for Root Chakra health.
- Examples: beans, lentils, nuts, seeds, eggs, tofu, fish, lean meats (depending on diet preference).
- Protein gives the body the sense of solidity and endurance, reinforcing the foundation of survival.
- **Practice:** Eat meals with balanced protein content, especially when feeling weak, anxious, or disconnected.

## Earthy Foods

- Foods with deep colors and earthy flavors resonate with Muladhara's vibration.
- Examples: red apples, cherries, pomegranates, dark leafy greens, whole grains, mushrooms.
- These foods not only support the body physically but also symbolically connect to the red, grounding frequency of the Root.

## Mindful Eating

The way food is consumed is as important as the food itself.

- Eat slowly and with gratitude.
- Savor the textures, colors, and flavors of each bite.
- Create rituals around eating that remind the body it is safe, cared for, and nourished.

## Affirmation While Eating

*"As I eat, I receive the earth's strength. My body is nourished, my roots are strong, my foundation is secure."*

Food therapy for Muladhara is not about restriction or rules but about **remembering food as earth's gift of survival.** By choosing grounding foods and eating with awareness, you fortify both body and spirit.

# Nature Practices: Forest Bathing, Gardening, Mountain Grounding

Because the Root Chakra is the energy of earth, the simplest and most profound way to balance it is to **reconnect directly with nature.** Natural environments restore nervous system balance, release stored stress, and remind us that we are part of the living web of life.

## Forest Bathing (Shinrin-yoku)

- Originating in Japan, forest bathing means immersing oneself in the atmosphere of the forest.
- The scent of trees, the sound of leaves, and the feel of earth underfoot all calm the Root Chakra. Science now shows that forest bathing lowers cortisol, boosts immunity, and promotes relaxation.
- **Practice:** Walk slowly and silently through a forest or wooded area. Breathe deeply, take in the sights and smells, and imagine each inhalation filling your Root with earth's vitality.

## Gardening

- Putting hands directly in soil awakens a primal sense of connection. Gardening mirrors the Root Chakra's symbolism of growth, nourishment, and cycles of life.
- Planting, watering, and harvesting are acts of grounding and survival — cultivating food and beauty from the earth.
- **Practice:** Spend time tending a garden, even a small container plant. As you work, silently repeat: *"I am one with the earth. What I nurture in her, she nurtures in me."*

## Mountain Grounding

- Mountains embody stability and permanence, serving as a mirror for Root energy. Sitting with or hiking in the mountains draws strength, resilience, and perspective.
- Their sheer size can shift fear into trust, reminding us of the enduring foundation beneath all life.
- **Practice:** Sit or stand at the base of a mountain or hillside. Close your eyes and imagine yourself as the mountain — tall, steady, immovable. Feel your Root Chakra expanding downward like bedrock.

## The Power of Nature Practices

Nature heals not by adding something foreign, but by **reminding us of what we already are**: grounded beings belonging to the earth. Forests, gardens, and mountains each offer their medicine — serenity, nourishment, and resilience. By immersing ourselves in them, we recharge Muladhara and rediscover safety, stability, and trust in life.

# Chapter 9 – Advanced Practitioner Applications

## Root Energy and Trauma Release

The Root Chakra is the energetic home of our most primal memories — not only personal experiences of safety and survival, but also ancestral and collective imprints of trauma. Because Muladhara develops in early childhood, unresolved fears or disruptions at this stage are often stored in the body as implicit memory. Practitioners working at this level must approach with **deep sensitivity, grounding, and awareness of trauma-informed care.**

### How Trauma Affects the Root

- **Hypervigilance:** The nervous system remains in constant alert mode, preventing full grounding.
- **Dissociation:** To escape pain, awareness "leaves" the body, weakening the Root's connection to earth.
- **Frozen Fear:** Survival energy becomes stuck in the lower body, manifesting as tension in hips, pelvis, and legs.

When the Root is impacted by trauma, clients may present with anxiety, panic attacks, digestive problems, chronic lower back pain, or difficulty feeling safe in relationships and environments.

## Energy Practices for Trauma Release

1. **Gentle Grounding Touch**
   Practitioners may place hands on or near the feet and ankles to invite energy downward without overwhelming the client. Gentle touch signals safety to the body and begins to rebuild Root stability.
2. **Slow Breath with Consent**
   Encouraging the client to place one hand on their belly while breathing deeply establishes self-regulation. Breath becomes a bridge between unconscious fear and conscious presence.
3. **Guided Visualization for Safety**
   Instead of immediately confronting traumatic images, clients are guided to imagine a safe, supportive place in nature (a tree, a cave, a mountain). This strengthens the Root's sense of inner refuge.
4. **Movement to Release Stuck Energy**
   Trauma is often "frozen" survival energy. Practices like shaking the legs, gentle stomping, or swaying the hips help discharge excess energy while re-establishing presence in the lower body.

## Practitioner Guidelines

- **Go Slowly:** Trauma release is not about forcing catharsis but creating conditions where safety allows the body to unwind naturally.
- **Work in Layers:** Begin with grounding, then move gently toward deeper layers of memory.
- **Empower the Client:** Encourage autonomy and choice. A safe Root experience is built when the client feels they have control.
- **Integrate:** Always close trauma-release sessions with grounding techniques (holding feet, breathing, or visualizing roots) so the client leaves stabilized.

## The Healing Path

Working with trauma in the Root is not only about healing the past — it is about **restoring the capacity to feel safe in the present.** When Muladhara is released from the grip of trauma, life force energy flows freely upward, enabling the higher chakras to awaken without fear.

# Hands-On Protocols for Grounding and Stabilizing Clients

For practitioners of Reiki, massage, acupressure, or other body-centered therapies, the Root Chakra requires a special approach. Because it is the center of survival and safety, hands-on protocols must emphasize **respect, boundaries, and consent** while providing the client with a profound sense of stability.

### Preparation for the Practitioner

- **Center Yourself First:** Before beginning, ground your own energy by standing barefoot, breathing into your lower belly, and visualizing roots descending into the earth. Clients sense the stability of the practitioner.
- **Set Intention:** Silently affirm: *"I create a safe space for grounding and healing."*
- **Establish Consent:** Because the Root area is intimate, always ask for clear permission and explain where hands will be placed or hovered.

### Basic Root Grounding Protocol

1. **Feet Hold**
   - Place your hands gently on or around the client's feet.

- o Imagine channeling stability into them, as though anchoring roots.
- o This alone can often stabilize energy and bring a scattered client back into presence.

2. **Leg Sweep**
   - o With both hands, slowly move from hips to feet, lightly brushing or hovering over the legs.
   - o This draws energy downward, releasing excess from the upper body.

3. **Hip Hold (Hover or Side Contact)**
   - o Place one hand gently on each side of the hips (or hover if more comfortable for the client).
   - o Visualize energy pooling into the pelvis, strengthening the Root Chakra's base.

4. **Lower Back Support**
   - o With the client lying face down, place hands over the sacrum and lower spine.
   - o Channel warmth and safety into this area, supporting release of fear and tension.

**Stabilizing Additions**

- **Foot Compression (Massage or Acupressure):** Gentle pressure at the soles grounds energy and reassures the nervous system.
- **Knee Hold:** Placing hands at the knees reinforces forward movement and stability.
- **Closing the Session:** Always finish by returning to the feet — either holding them firmly or pressing gently — to "seal" the grounding.

Key Principles

- **Safety First:** The Root Chakra can store trauma. Always proceed slowly, watch for signs of discomfort, and invite the client to speak up if anything feels overwhelming.

- **Containment Over Expansion:** At the Root, less is more. Focus on stabilizing energy before encouraging flow upward.
- **Empowerment:** Invite the client to visualize roots, affirm safety, or breathe deeply during the protocol. This reinforces self-agency in their grounding process.

**Affirmation for Practitioner and Client:**
*"I am safe, I am supported, I belong to the earth. My roots are strong and steady."*

# The Role of Muladhara in Remote Healing

Energy knows no boundaries of time or space. Just as Reiki and other energy modalities can be shared across distance, so too can the stabilizing power of the Root Chakra be accessed and harmonized remotely. Because Muladhara governs safety and survival, remote work with this chakra must emphasize **clear intention, strong grounding from the practitioner, and careful containment of energy.**

**Unique Challenges of Remote Root Work**

- **Safety at a Distance:** Clients may feel vulnerable when opening their Root energy without the physical reassurance of a practitioner present.
- **Disconnection from the Body:** Because Muladhara is tied to physicality, it can be harder for some clients to sense grounding when not physically touched.
- **Energetic Containment:** Without proper closure, a client may feel spacey or ungrounded after a remote session.

**Practitioner Preparation**

1. **Ground Yourself First:** Before beginning, connect deeply with the earth. Visualize roots anchoring your own energy so that you transmit stability to the client.
2. **Create Sacred Space:** Use ritual — light a candle, place grounding stones, or diffuse earthy oils — to establish a strong energetic container.
3. **Call in Protection:** Intentionally invoke guides, Reiki symbols, or prayer for the client's safety.

## Remote Healing Protocol for Muladhara

1. **Establish Connection:**
   o Invite the client to sit or lie comfortably with feet touching the ground or floor.
   o Have them place one hand on their lower belly and the other on their heart for self-contact.
2. **Send Grounding Energy:**
   o Focus your intention at the base of their spine, visualizing red light radiating downward into the earth.
   o Use Reiki symbols (Cho Ku Rei for power, Sei He Ki for emotional harmony) or visualized roots to transmit safety.
3. **Stabilize Through the Feet:**
   o Imagine holding their feet in your hands, channeling warmth and security.
   o Visualize heavy energy draining through their soles into the earth, replaced by strength and calm.
4. **Affirm Safety:**
   o Silently or aloud, repeat affirmations such as: *"You are safe. You are grounded. The earth supports you."*
5. **Close and Seal:**
   o Imagine wrapping a cocoon of grounding energy around their lower body.
   o End by anchoring them back into their physical environment — encouraging them to touch the floor, drink water, or eat something nourishing.

## Best Practices

- Always give clients grounding instructions **before and after** remote sessions.
- Encourage them to stay present in their body by noticing sensations, sounds, or breath.

- Follow up after the session to ensure they feel stable and supported.

**The Hidden Gift of Remote Root Healing**
Working with Muladhara remotely teaches both practitioner and client that grounding is not dependent on physical contact. The true foundation lies in **intention, presence, and the ever-available support of the earth.** Distance only amplifies the lesson that stability and safety begin within.

# Clearing Ancestral Fear and Karmic Imprints

The Root Chakra is not only the foundation of individual survival — it is also the **storehouse of ancestral memory and karmic residue.** Through Muladhara, we carry the survival experiences of our bloodline, as well as karmic lessons from previous incarnations. Practitioners working at this depth engage with energy that extends beyond the personal, entering collective and transgenerational fields.

**Ancestral Fear in the Root**

- Families and communities that endured **war, famine, migration, or displacement** often pass survival fears forward.
- Even when present-day circumstances are stable, descendants may carry unexplained anxiety, scarcity mindsets, or difficulty feeling safe.
- These imprints live in the lower body — the hips, pelvis, legs, and spine — creating patterns of instability that repeat across generations.

## Karmic Root Imprints

- Past-life traumas tied to survival (loss of home, persecution, poverty) can surface as phobias, chronic insecurity, or fear of belonging.
- Karmic lessons often repeat until they are consciously integrated: a soul may incarnate in similar survival conditions to learn resilience, trust, and grounding.
- The Root becomes the chakra where these karmic tests are most vividly experienced.

## Practitioner Methods for Clearing

1. **Ancestral Visualization**
   - Guide clients to imagine standing in a long line of ancestors, roots from their body intertwining with those who came before.
   - Invite them to send healing light down the line, dissolving fear and anchoring safety for both past and future generations.
2. **Symbolic Release Rituals**
   - Encourage clients to write ancestral fears (scarcity, abandonment, persecution) on paper, then bury or burn them as an offering to the earth.
   - This act grounds karmic release in the material world, completing cycles of fear.
3. **Karmic Regression Work**
   - With consent, some practitioners guide clients into meditative journeys or past-life regressions, identifying survival-based traumas.
   - Once revealed, healing can occur through forgiveness, re-parenting the past self, or sending Reiki to the moment of trauma.
4. **Body-Based Ancestral Clearing**
   - Trauma often anchors in the hips and legs. Through breath, movement (like shaking or

stomping), and touch, these stored imprints can be discharged, freeing the lineage from holding fear in the Root.

### Affirmations for Ancestral Healing

- *"I honor the survival of those before me, and I release what is not mine to carry."*
- *"The strength of my ancestors supports me, and their fears no longer bind me."*
- *"I am safe in this lifetime. I root into the earth with trust."*

### The Deeper Gift

Clearing ancestral and karmic imprints does not erase history — it transforms it. By healing Muladhara, we shift the legacy of fear into one of resilience. The healed Root not only stabilizes the individual but also **frees future generations** to live from a place of belonging, trust, and love.

# Cross-Referencing with TCM Meridians: Kidney and Bladder

The Root Chakra's themes of survival, vitality, and grounding resonate strongly with **Traditional Chinese Medicine (TCM)**, especially the **Kidney** and **Bladder meridians**. Just as Muladhara is considered the energetic foundation of the chakra system, the Kidneys are seen in TCM as the **"Root of Life."** This cross-referencing offers practitioners a broader perspective for integrating Eastern energy systems in holistic care.

## Kidney Meridian – The Root of Essence

- **Location:** Begins at the sole of the foot (Kidney 1, *Yongquan*), travels up the inner leg, and connects through the lower abdomen.
- **Function:** In TCM, the Kidneys store **Jing** (essence), the fundamental energy inherited at birth that governs vitality, growth, and longevity.
- **Connection to Muladhara:**
  - The Kidneys provide the foundation of Yin–Yang balance, mirroring Muladhara's role as the grounding base of all chakras.
  - Fear, the primary emotion of Kidney imbalance, directly parallels Root Chakra instability.
  - Practices that strengthen Kidney Qi — warming foods, herbal tonics, acupressure — support Root Chakra vitality.

*Practitioner Insight:* Working with Kidney 1 (the "Bubbling Spring" point) is especially grounding. Applying acupressure or Reiki to the soles of the feet helps anchor energy, calm fear, and stabilize the Root.

## Bladder Meridian – Release and Flow

- **Location:** Runs along the back of the body, with two parallel channels on either side of the spine, connecting strongly to the sacrum and legs.
- **Function:** The Bladder system governs fluid balance, the release of toxins, and the nervous system. It also interacts with Kidney energy to regulate survival and vitality.
- **Connection to Muladhara:**
  - Chronic tension in the lower back, hips, or legs (often signs of Root imbalance) corresponds to Bladder meridian blockages.

- The Bladder meridian also stores unresolved fear and trauma along the spine, echoing Muladhara's imprinting of survival stress.
- Techniques like acupressure along Bladder 23 (*Shenshu*) or Bladder 52 (*Zhishi*) can support grounding, resilience, and Root healing.

## Practical Integration

- **Energy Mapping:** When a client presents with Root Chakra issues (fear, instability, lower body pain), check Kidney and Bladder meridian imbalances as a complementary perspective.
- **Combined Practices:**
  - Reiki or chakra healing at the Root + acupressure at Kidney 1.
  - Lower back massage or cupping along the Bladder meridian to release stored Root trauma.
  - Breathing into the lower dantian (below the navel) to strengthen both the Root Chakra and Kidney Qi.

## Shared Wisdom

- **Muladhara ↔ Kidneys:** Both are the "storehouses" of life force, tied to survival and fear.
- **Root ↔ Bladder Meridian:** Both regulate grounding, elimination, and release of excess tension.
- Together, these systems affirm the truth that survival is not only about the physical body — it is about the harmony of energy flow between earth, body, and spirit.

# Grounding Synchronization: Aligning Practitioner and Client

When working with Muladhara, the practitioner's own state of grounding profoundly influences the client. The Root Chakra responds instinctively to the energy field of others; if the practitioner is calm, present, and rooted, the client naturally entrains to that vibration. If the practitioner is ungrounded, anxious, or scattered, the session may reinforce instability instead of healing.

This is why **grounding synchronization** — aligning practitioner and client energies into a shared state of safety and stability — is a cornerstone of advanced Root Chakra practice.

**Why Synchronization Matters**

- **Energetic Entrainment:** Just as heartbeats can synchronize in close proximity, subtle energy fields harmonize when two people share intentional space.
- **Felt Safety:** Clients often "borrow" the practitioner's nervous system regulation. If you are grounded, they can feel safe enough to release.
- **Clear Channeling:** Synchronization ensures that the practitioner is not projecting fear or imbalance into the session.

**Practitioner Preparation**

1. **Root Yourself First:** Before meeting the client, breathe deeply into your belly, visualize roots anchoring from your feet into the earth, and affirm: *"I am steady. I am safe. I am present."*
2. **Check for Alignment:** Notice any personal stress or agitation. Address it with breathwork, grounding oils, or quick movement before beginning.

3.  **Enter with Intention:** As you step into the healing space, silently affirm your role as a grounded, stable presence.

## Synchronization Techniques

1.  **Shared Breathwork**
    o   Invite the client to place one hand on their belly.
    o   Breathe together slowly, inhaling for 4 counts, exhaling for 6–8 counts.
    o   This calms both nervous systems and roots energy downward.
2.  **Mirroring Body Position**
    o   Sit or stand in a grounded posture, feet firmly planted.
    o   Encourage the client to do the same. Subtle mirroring communicates safety without words.
3.  **Energetic Linking**
    o   Visualize a shared cord of red light connecting your Root Chakra to the client's.
    o   Imagine this cord descending into the earth, anchoring both of you into the same foundation.
4.  **Closing Synchronization**
    o   End by returning to the feet — holding, hovering, or visualizing them firmly planted.
    o   Invite the client to take a deep breath and notice the steadiness in their body.

## Key Considerations

*   **Boundaries:** Synchronization is alignment, not merging. Stay grounded in your own Root while guiding the client toward theirs.
*   **Ethics of Presence:** The more authentic your groundedness, the more effective the session. Pretending calm cannot substitute for true stability.

- **Integration:** Encourage clients to anchor themselves after the session with water, food, or movement, ensuring the grounding continues beyond your shared field.

**Practitioner's Affirmation Before Synchronization:**
*"I stand rooted in the earth. I offer stability, safety, and presence. May my grounding support my client's grounding."*

# Chapter 10 – Transformation Through Muladhara

## Case Studies: Overcoming Fear, Restoring Safety, Rebuilding Stability

Healing the Root Chakra is not an abstract idea — it is a lived, embodied transformation. When Muladhara shifts from fear to trust, individuals rediscover their ability to stand firmly in the world. The following case studies illustrate how Root healing manifests in practice, showing the pathway from instability to stability, from survival to grounded thriving.

### CASE STUDY 1 – OVERCOMING FEAR

*Client Profile:* A young professional in her 30s, struggling with chronic anxiety and panic attacks. Despite having financial stability and supportive relationships, she felt constant dread of losing everything.

*Root Chakra Imbalance:* Fear and insecurity rooted in childhood instability and ancestral experiences of migration. Energetic assessment revealed tension in the lower spine and legs, with blocked flow at Muladhara.

*Healing Approach:*

- Weekly Reiki sessions focusing on feet, hips, and sacrum.
- Grounding visualizations (tree roots meditation) as daily homework.
- Ancestral release ritual to honor and let go of inherited fear.

*Outcome:* Within three months, panic attacks diminished significantly. The client reported a newfound sense of safety and the ability to make decisions without fear of collapse. She described it as *"finally feeling the earth beneath me."*

## CASE STUDY 2 – RESTORING SAFETY

*Client Profile:* A man in his 40s who survived a traumatic car accident. Though physically healed, he felt restless, had difficulty sleeping, and avoided driving altogether.

*Root Chakra Imbalance:* The accident had disrupted his sense of bodily safety. Muladhara was holding trauma in the hips and sacrum, manifesting as tension, nightmares, and avoidance behaviors.

*Healing Approach:*

- Trauma-informed bodywork focusing on the lower back and legs.
- Gentle movement practices (walking barefoot, stomping) to discharge stuck fear.
- Sound healing with the LAM mantra and low-frequency drumming to re-pattern safety.

*Outcome:* Over time, his sleep improved, and his nightmares subsided. Gradual exposure, paired with grounding rituals, allowed him to return to driving without panic. He described the process as *"finding my footing in the world again."*

## CASE STUDY 3 – REBUILDING STABILITY

*Client Profile:* A woman in her late 50s going through divorce and financial upheaval. She reported feeling unmoored, "like the ground had been pulled out from under her."

*Root Chakra Imbalance:* Loss of home, financial security, and partnership had destabilized Muladhara. Energy was scattered, with symptoms of fatigue, digestive upset, and difficulty concentrating.

*Healing Approach:*

- Nutritional grounding with root vegetables and protein-rich meals.
- Regular Reiki treatments emphasizing Root, Sacral, and Solar Plexus alignment.
- Creating new "earth rituals" such as gardening and mountain meditation.
- Affirmations: *"I belong to myself. The earth supports me in rebuilding."*

*Outcome:* Over six months, she cultivated a renewed sense of stability. She secured housing, began a new career path, and reported, *"I don't just survive anymore. I feel rooted in myself."*

## The Pattern of Transformation

These cases show that Root healing always begins with **safety and presence.** From there, fear softens, trauma releases, and life force returns. Each person's path may look different, but the transformation always carries the same essence: **to stand, to trust, and to root into life once more.**

# Practitioner Stories of Root Chakra Breakthroughs

While client case studies show the personal impact of Root Chakra healing, practitioner experiences reveal the deeper wisdom that emerges when working with Muladhara. These stories illustrate how breakthroughs often occur in unexpected ways, teaching both healer and client that grounding is as much about presence as it is about technique.

## STORY 1 – THE BREAKTHROUGH OF STILLNESS

*A Reiki Master shares:*

"I had a client who couldn't sit still — she was always fidgeting, anxious, unable to breathe deeply. Instead of trying to push energy through the Root, I simply held her feet for what felt like a long time. Eventually, she sighed and whispered, *'I feel like I've landed for the first time in years.'* That moment reminded me that sometimes, the simplest touch at the Root — holding presence — is the most powerful healing."

## STORY 2 – WHEN ANCESTRAL FEAR RELEASED

*A shamanic practitioner recalls:*

"During a journey session, I saw images of my client's ancestors fleeing war. She had been living with unexplainable fear her whole life. We honored those ancestors, thanking them for survival, and then released the fear back into the earth. The client later said, *'I don't feel like I'm running anymore.'* It was a turning point for me as a practitioner — realizing how much of the Root we carry for those who came before."

## STORY 3 – GROUNDING AFTER SHOCK

*A massage therapist describes:*

"One client came to me after a sudden job loss. She said she felt like her legs didn't belong to her body. I worked slowly along her calves, knees, and hips, always inviting her to breathe into each area. By the end, she stood up taller and said, *'I feel like I can stand on my own two feet again.'* For me, it was a reminder that Root work restores dignity as much as energy."

## STORY 4 – THE PRACTITIONER'S OWN HEALING

*A yoga teacher reflects:*

"For years, I was teaching grounding practices but secretly living with my own instability. When I finally committed to barefoot walks every morning, eating more root vegetables, and chanting LAM daily, I realized: my teaching changed because my Root changed. The students could feel it. Sometimes, our own Root breakthroughs are what truly empower our work with others."

**The Practitioner's Wisdom**

These stories show that Root Chakra breakthroughs are not only about clients — they are about the **mutual journey of healer and healed.** Muladhara teaches humility, patience, and presence. Every breakthrough affirms that grounding is not a quick fix but a steady practice of safety, trust, and belonging.

# The Ripple Effect: How Grounding Supports the Whole Energy System

The chakras do not operate in isolation. They are an interwoven network, like rivers flowing into one another. When the Root Chakra is balanced, its stability ripples upward, strengthening and harmonizing the entire energy system. Conversely, when it is unstable, higher chakras cannot fully expand. Healing Muladhara is therefore not only about survival — it is about empowering the full journey of consciousness.

## From Root to Sacral (Creativity and Pleasure)

When safety is restored in the Root, the Sacral Chakra feels free to open. Pleasure, intimacy, and creative flow can only thrive when the body knows it is secure. Without grounding, creativity becomes scattered; with grounding, it blossoms into joyful expression.

## From Root to Solar Plexus (Confidence and Will)

A strong Root creates the foundation for Manipura, the center of confidence and action. When survival fears no longer dominate, personal willpower emerges naturally. Decisions are clearer, self-esteem steadier, and the ability to move forward more resilient.

## From Root to Heart (Love and Connection)

The bridge between Root and Heart is perhaps the most transformative ripple. Grounding allows love to expand without fear. Relationships become anchored in trust rather than dependency, and compassion radiates from a foundation of inner safety.

## From Root to Throat (Expression and Truth)

An unstable Root often silences the voice. When the body is grounded, the Throat Chakra feels secure enough to express truth. Words gain weight and authenticity because they rise from a steady foundation.

## From Root to Third Eye (Vision and Intuition)

Higher perception requires a body that is firmly rooted. Without grounding, visions become fantasies or illusions. With grounding, intuition is clear, reliable, and practical — guidance that can be acted upon in the real world.

## From Root to Crown (Spiritual Connection)

Muladhara is the soil in which the Crown blossoms. True spiritual awakening is not an escape from the body, but an embodiment of spirit in matter. A grounded Root allows the Crown to open safely, so that expanded states of consciousness are integrated, not destabilizing.

## The Systemic Truth

When the Root Chakra is healed, **every chakra benefits.** Grounding is the silent support behind creativity, confidence, love, expression, vision, and connection to the divine. Stability at Muladhara is like the steady drumbeat that keeps the entire symphony of the chakras in harmony.

# Chapter 11 – Reflection & Integration

## Daily Self-Care Rituals for Root Strength

The Root Chakra thrives on **consistency and simplicity.** While profound healing sessions and deep spiritual practices are valuable, it is the small, repeated actions of daily life that keep Muladhara strong. Creating a routine of grounding rituals signals to the body: *"You are safe. You are supported. You belong."*

**Morning Grounding Breath**

- Before rising from bed, place your hands on your lower belly.
- Inhale deeply, feeling your belly expand. Exhale slowly, imagining your breath sinking down into the earth.
- Repeat for 3–5 cycles, affirming: *"I begin this day grounded and secure."*

**Barefoot Connection**

- Spend a few minutes each day walking barefoot on natural ground — grass, soil, or stone.
- As you walk, visualize roots extending from your feet into the earth.
- This ritual recharges Muladhara with the earth's electromagnetic field and reminds you of your belonging.

## Root Affirmations

- Speak simple affirmations aloud while looking into a mirror:
  - *"I am safe."*
  - *"I am grounded."*
  - *"The earth supports me."*
- Repetition builds new neural pathways of safety and stability.

## Grounding Foods

- Incorporate root vegetables, protein, or earthy teas (ginger, dandelion, licorice) into daily meals.
- Bless your food with gratitude before eating, acknowledging it as earth's gift.

## Evening Release Ritual

- Before sleep, sit quietly and visualize any stress, fear, or worry draining down through your feet into the earth.
- Imagine red light at your Root Chakra glowing steadily as you rest.
- End with a simple mantra: *"I am safe to let go and sleep."*

## Weekly Nature Check-In

- At least once a week, spend intentional time in nature — a forest walk, gardening, or sitting at the base of a tree.
- Journal afterward: *How did I feel before? How do I feel now?*
- Notice how natural grounding shifts your energy.

**The Wisdom of Ritual:**
Small daily practices are the bricks that build a strong foundation. By tending to Muladhara each day, you train the body to live in trust rather than fear, and you weave grounding into the fabric of your life.

# Journaling Prompts for Safety, Trust, and Belonging

Writing is one of the most powerful tools for Root Chakra integration. By putting thoughts and feelings onto paper, we create a dialogue with the subconscious, allowing hidden fears and forgotten strengths to surface. The following prompts invite reflection on Muladhara's core themes: **safety, trust, and belonging.**

**Prompts for Safety**

- When in my life have I felt the safest? What circumstances or people contributed to that feeling?
- What situations trigger feelings of unsafety in me now? Are these threats real, or echoes of past experiences?
- What does *being safe in my body* mean to me? How can I cultivate more of that daily?

**Prompts for Trust**

- Who or what do I instinctively trust? How do I know?
- Where do I find it hardest to trust — in myself, in others, or in life? Why?
- Write about a time when trusting led to growth or healing, even if it felt risky.
- If my Root Chakra could speak, what would it say about trusting the earth and my foundation?

## Prompts for Belonging

- Where do I feel most at home — in a place, with people, or within myself?
- Write about a time you felt excluded. How did it affect your sense of grounding?
- What does belonging mean to me beyond community — belonging to the earth, to my lineage, or to existence itself?
- If I truly believed I belonged here, how would I live differently?

## Integration Practice

Choose one prompt each morning or evening. Set a timer for 10 minutes and write without stopping to edit or judge. Allow your subconscious to speak freely. Over time, these reflections will reveal patterns — both the fears that weaken the Root and the strengths that anchor you.

# Guided Exercise: Creating a Foundation-Centered Life Mantra

A mantra is more than words — it is a vibration that reshapes consciousness. For the Root Chakra, a life mantra becomes an anchor, reminding you of your foundation even when life feels uncertain. This exercise will guide you to create your own personal affirmation that centers on safety, trust, and belonging.

## Step 1 – Identify Core Needs

Ask yourself: *What do I most need to feel safe and grounded?* Examples: stability, support, connection, trust, strength. Write down one or two words that resonate.

Step 2 – Transform into Positive Presence

Turn those needs into affirmations of presence:

- "I am stable."
- "I am supported."
- "I am safe."
  Choose wording that feels empowering, as though it is already true.

## Step 3 – Anchor to the Root

Bring awareness to the base of your spine. Place a hand on your lower belly.

- Inhale deeply.
- As you exhale, speak your chosen words slowly, imagining them vibrating in Muladhara.
  Repeat 3–7 times, letting the mantra sink into your foundation.

## Step 4 – Create Your Mantra

Now, weave your affirmations into one flowing statement. Examples:

- *"I am safe, I belong, and the earth supports me."*
- *"I root deeply, I trust fully, I live freely."*
- *"The foundation of my life is stability, strength, and love."*

## Step 5 – Daily Practice

- **Morning:** Speak your mantra aloud before starting your day.
- **During Stress:** Repeat it silently to bring your energy back to the Root.

- **Evening:** Whisper it before bed to calm your body and anchor restful sleep.

**Tip:** Write your mantra in a journal, on a sticky note by your mirror, or even create a small piece of art with the words. The more you see and speak it, the more it becomes part of your energetic reality.

# Chapter 12 – Quick Reference Toolkit

## Practitioner Cheat-Sheet: Root-Focused Reiki Sessions

This quick guide is designed for Reiki and energy practitioners who want a structured yet flexible approach to balancing Muladhara. It distills key hand positions, protocols, and grounding techniques into a **session-ready reference**.

**Session Goals**

- Anchor the client in the present moment.
- Clear fear, instability, or survival stress from Muladhara.
- Restore stability, vitality, and a sense of belonging.
- Ground the client before closing the session.

**Hand Positions**

- **Feet:** Begin or end here. Place hands on/over soles to ground and anchor.
- **Ankles/Calves:** Stabilize energy flow down the legs.
- **Hips/Pelvis:** Balance left/right channels; work gently with survival stress.
- **Lower Back/Sacrum:** Release stored tension, fear, and trauma at the base of the spine.

*Tip: Always explain hand placement in advance, respecting boundaries. Hovering hands can be just as effective.*

## Symbols & Techniques (for Reiki Level II and above)

- **Cho Ku Rei (Power Symbol):** Strengthen and stabilize Root energy.
- **Sei He Ki (Harmony Symbol):** Address emotional fear, trauma, and instability.
- **Dai Ko Myo (Master Symbol):** Bring deep spiritual grounding, especially in ancestral or karmic work.

## Session Flow

1. **Ground Yourself First:** Center, breathe, and root your own energy before touching the client.
2. **Opening Anchor:** Begin at the feet, visualizing roots extending into the earth.
3. **Root Clearing:** Place or hover hands at the sacrum, hips, or pelvis. Send Reiki until warmth or pulsing is felt.
4. **Balance Left/Right:** Sweep energy down each leg to ensure even grounding.
5. **Seal and Close:** Always return to the feet, holding firmly until the client feels steady.

## Grounding Add-Ons

- **Sound:** Chant LAM or use a low-frequency drum/bowl during sacral/hip work.
- **Crystals:** Place hematite, red jasper, or smoky quartz near the feet or hips.
- **Oils:** Diffuse vetiver or cedarwood during the session for added depth.

## Closing Affirmations (suggested to share with client)

- *"I am safe in my body."*
- *"The earth supports me fully."*
- *"My foundation is strong, steady, and secure."*

This cheat-sheet provides the **bare essentials** for Root-focused Reiki sessions while allowing practitioners to adapt based on client needs, intuition, and boundaries.

# Daily 5-Minute Grounding Routine

This short sequence can be practiced anytime — morning, during stress, or before bed. It combines breath, body, and intention to stabilize Muladhara quickly and effectively.

### Step 1 – Rooted Breath (1 minute)

- Sit or stand with feet flat on the floor.
- Place one hand on your lower belly.
- Inhale slowly through the nose, expanding the belly.
- Exhale through the mouth, imagining your breath sinking down into the earth.
- Repeat for 5–6 deep breaths.

### Step 2 – Foot Connection (1 minute)

- Press your feet firmly into the ground.
- Imagine roots extending downward from your soles, spreading wide and deep.
- With each exhale, release fear or tension into the earth; with each inhale, draw stability upward.

### Step 3 – Stomping or Gentle Movement (1 minute)

- Stomp your feet gently on the ground, or sway your hips side to side.
- Feel the vibration travel up your legs into your spine.
- This awakens the Root and discharges stagnant energy.

### Step 4 – Visualization of Red Light (1 minute)

- Close your eyes and imagine a glowing red light at the base of your spine.
- See it pulsing steadily, spreading warmth into your legs and feet.
- Affirm: *"I am safe. I am grounded. I belong."*

### Step 5 – Seal the Practice (1 minute)

- Place your hands over your heart and belly together.
- Take three deep breaths, feeling the connection between Root (safety) and Heart (love).
- Smile gently, anchoring this balance before continuing your day.

### Quick Mantra for Daily Use:
*"With every breath, I root into the earth. With every step, I stand in safety and strength."*

# Conclusion: Living Through the Root

The Root Chakra is more than an energy center — it is the foundation of our human experience. It is where spirit meets matter, where the soul chooses embodiment, and where our journey through the chakras begins. Every lesson of Muladhara reminds us of one timeless truth: before we can expand upward, we must first root downward.

Living through the Root means honoring survival, safety, and stability as sacred. It means recognizing that fear is not an enemy but a messenger, pointing us back toward trust. It means remembering that the body is not separate from spirit — it is the temple through which our spirit expresses itself.

When Muladhara is strong, we walk differently in the world.

- We no longer move from fear but from presence.
- We no longer chase belonging but know we already belong.
- We no longer seek safety outside ourselves but cultivate it within.

A balanced Root creates ripples through the entire chakra system: creativity flows freely, confidence grows naturally, love expands generously, expression becomes authentic, vision sharpens clearly, and spiritual connection deepens profoundly. The foundation steadies the tower; the roots nourish the tree; Muladhara anchors the soul.

But perhaps the greatest gift of the Root is its simplicity. Grounding does not require rare initiations or elaborate rituals. It happens in the ordinary: bare feet on the earth, the rhythm of breath, the stillness of a mountain, the steadiness of a meal shared with gratitude. By returning again and again to these simple practices, we live in alignment with Muladhara's wisdom.

As you close this book, carry with you the remembrance that you are always supported. The earth beneath you has never failed; it holds you still. Each step you take is both a rooting and a rising — the dance of survival and spirit entwined.

**Living through the Root is living as a whole: grounded in the earth, open to love, and ready to rise.**

# Bibliography

## CLASSICAL & YOGIC SOURCES

- Feuerstein, Georg. *The Yoga Tradition: Its History, Literature, Philosophy, and Practice.* Hohm Press, 2001.
- Avalon, Arthur (Sir John Woodroffe). *The Serpent Power: The Secrets of Tantric and Shaktic Yoga.* Dover Publications, 1974.
- Swami Sivananda. *The Chakras.* Divine Life Society, 1994.
- Upanishads (trans. Eknath Easwaran). *The Upanishads.* Nilgiri Press, 2007.

## CHAKRA & ENERGY HEALING WORKS

- Judith, Anodea. *Wheels of Life: A User's Guide to the Chakra System.* Llewellyn Publications, 1987.
- Myss, Caroline. *Anatomy of the Spirit.* Harmony Books, 1996.
- Brennan, Barbara Ann. *Hands of Light: A Guide to Healing Through the Human Energy Field.* Bantam, 1988.
- Sills, Franklyn. *Foundations in Craniosacral Biodynamics: The Breath of Life and Fundamental Skills.* North Atlantic Books, 2012.

## REIKI & SPIRITUAL HEALING

- Takata, Hawayo. *Reiki: Hawayo Takata's Story.* Reiki Alliance, 1998.

- Petter, Frank Arjava. *This Is Reiki: Transformation of Body, Mind and Soul from the Origins to the Practice.* Lotus Press, 2012.
- Rand, William Lee. *Reiki: The Healing Touch.* Vision Publications, 1991.

## CROSS-CULTURAL & MYSTICAL REFERENCES

- Halevi, Z'ev ben Shimon. *Kabbalah: Tradition of Hidden Knowledge.* Thames & Hudson, 1991.
- Hanh, Thich Nhat. *Peace Is Every Step.* Bantam, 1992.
- Ibn Arabi. *Journey to the Lord of Power.* Inner Traditions, 1981.
- Underhill, Evelyn. *Mysticism: A Study in the Nature and Development of Spiritual Consciousness.* Dover Publications, 2002.

## MODERN SCIENCE & RESEARCH

- McCraty, Rollin, et al. *Science of the Heart: Exploring the Role of the Heart in Human Performance.* HeartMath Institute, 2015.
- Childre, Doc, and Howard Martin. *The HeartMath Solution.* HarperOne, 1999.
- Pert, Candace B. *Molecules of Emotion: The Science Behind Mind-Body Medicine.* Scribner, 1997.
- Lipton, Bruce H. *The Biology of Belief.* Hay House, 2005.

## ADDITIONAL RESOURCES

- Eden, Donna. *Energy Medicine.* TarcherPerigee, 2008.
- Osho. *The Book of Secrets: 112 Meditations to Discover the Mystery Within.* St. Martin's Griffin, 1998.
- Chopra, Deepak. *Quantum Healing.* Bantam, 19

# Message From The Author

When I first began exploring the chakras many years ago, I was immediately drawn to the brilliance of the upper centers — intuition, vision, and spiritual awakening. Like many seekers, I wanted to rise, to reach upward toward light and transcendence. But in time I discovered what every true teacher of this path eventually learns: we cannot rise safely until we root deeply.

The **Root Chakra, Muladhara,** is where it all begins. It is the ground beneath our feet, the safety within our body, the foundation upon which every other energy center rests. Without it, no amount of meditation, spiritual practice, or healing work can remain steady. This truth has revealed itself to me again and again, both in my personal journey and in the work I've shared with students and clients around the world.

In this book, I've sought to honor both the **ancient teachings** of Muladhara — its mantras, symbols, and esoteric wisdom — and the **modern applications** that make it a practical tool for daily life. From yogic traditions to Western psychology, from ancestral healing to somatic grounding practices, Muladhara has always taught one timeless lesson: *you are safe when you remember your connection to the earth.*

As you read, you may notice echoes of your own story — moments of fear, instability, or disconnection — as well as glimmers of strength, endurance, and belonging. My hope is that these pages not only inform you but also guide you back into your body, back into your roots, and back into trust.

May this book remind you that survival is not merely about getting through — it is about **thriving with stability, security,**

**and strength.** And may it be a foundation not only for your spiritual practice but also for your life — steadying your steps as you walk your unique path.

With grounding, compassion, and gratitude,
**Dr. Constance Santego**

# About the Author

**Dr. Constance Santego, Ph.D., DNM** is an award-winning author, teacher, and natural medicine doctor who has dedicated

more than 25 years to the study and practice of energy healing. A Grand Reiki Master and founder of multiple wellness and educational programs, she has trained thousands of students worldwide in Reiki, holistic therapies, and intuitive development.

Her passion is to bring ancient wisdom into practical, modern tools that anyone can use for healing and self-discovery. She has authored more than forty books, ranging from the *Reiki*

*Wisdom* series and *Secrets of a Healer* guides to spiritual fiction exploring the Nine Spiritual Gifts. Her teaching blends Eastern philosophies, Western natural medicine, and modern energy science — always with compassion at the center.

Dr. Santego's mission is to help people connect with their inner wisdom, awaken their intuitive gifts, and live with greater balance, joy, and love. When she is not writing or teaching, she enjoys life in British Columbia, surrounded by nature's beauty, which continues to inspire her work.

# ALSO AVAILABLE

For additional information on

Constance Santego's

wide range of Motivational Products, Coaching Sessions,
Spiritual Retreats,
Live Events and Educational Programs

Go to

www.ConstanceSantego.ca

Follow on Instagram - Constance_Santego and
Facebook - constancesantegoo

Subscribe and receive Free Information and Meditations on her
YouTube Channel - Constance Santego

## Secrets of a Healer, Magic of Reiki

ISBN: 978-1-7772220-0-0

.

www.ingramcontent.com/pod-product-compliance
Lightning Source LLC
Chambersburg PA
CBHW071748120626
46550CB00002B/713

*9 7 8 1 9 9 0 0 6 2 9 4 0 *